# STRATEGIES FOR RESEARCH
## in Constructivist International Relations

AUDIE KLOTZ AND CECELIA LYNCH

*M.E.Sharpe*
Armonk, New York
London, England

**Library of Congress Cataloging-in-Publication Data**

Klotz, Audie, 1962-
Strategies for research in constructivist international relations / by Audie Klotz and
Cecelia Lynch.
    p. cm. — (International relations in a constructed world)
Includes bibliographical references and index.
 ISBN-13: 978-0-7656-2023-1 (cloth : alk. paper) —ISBN 978-0-7656-2024-8 (pbk.: alk. paper)
 1. International relations—Research. 2. Constructivism (Philosophy) 3. Research—
Methodology. I. Lynch, Cecelia. II. Title.

JZ1308.K56 2007
327.1072—dc22                                                                               2006032192

Printed in the United States of America

| BM (c) | 10 | 9 | 8 | 7 | 6 | 5 | 4 | 3 | 2 | 1 |
| --- | --- | --- | --- | --- | --- | --- | --- | --- | --- | --- |
| BM (p) | 10 | 9 | 8 | 7 | 6 | 5 | 4 | 3 | 2 | 1 |

# Contents

# Acknowledgments

Completing this project took much longer than we initially expected. During that time, we have benefited enormously from—and continue to wrestle with—superb comments from many friends and colleagues. Most read one or another version of the manuscript, and a few did so more than once. Others participated in seminars and conference panels where we presented portions of this work. We also received feedback from classroom testing, including direct responses from students. Braden Smith provided invaluable assistance with copy editing, formatting, and indexing. The hospitality of our families made this cross-country endeavor enjoyable!

At the risk of overlooking someone, we wish to thank all of the following people for their insights and encouragement. Of course, none of them are responsible for any unresolved tensions, infelicitous phrases, or controversial readings of the literature. Emanuel Adler (and his students), Hayward Alker, Sammy Barkin (and his students), Michael Barnett, Francis Beer, Tom Berger, Janice Bially Mattern, Dave Black, Thomas Boellstorff, Mike Bosia, Michele Budz, Heike Brabandt, Alison Brysk, Walter Carlsnaes, Jeff Checkel, Catia Confortini, Paul D'Anieri, Stephanie DiAlto, Jack Donnelly, Roxanne Doty, John Duffield, Bud Duvall, David Easton, Steve Engelmann, Erik Faleski, Karin Fierke, Marty Finnemore, Brian Fisher, Mervyn Frost (and his students), Chandra Gerber, Patti Goff, Dan Green (and his students), Siba Grovogui, Stefano Guzzini, Rod Hall, Roger Haydon, Jason Hsu, Helen Ingram, Celine Jacquemin, Nathan Jones, Peter Katzenstein (and his students), Beth Kier (and her students), Paul Kowert, Fritz Kratochwil, Henrik Larsen, Bill Maurer, Michael Loriaux, Kevin McGahan, Himadeep Muppidi, Philip Nel, Daniel Nexon, Kim Nossal, Cindy O'Hagan, Nick Onuf, Saba Ozyurt, Simon Reich, Wayne Sandholtz, Hans Peter Schmitz, Susan Sell (and her students), Mara Sidney, Michael

Simon, Duncan Snidal, Etel Solingen, Dorothy Solinger, Michael Struett, Mira Sucharov, Ann Tickner, Jacqui True, Robert Uriu (and his students), Katja Weber, Alex Wendt, Antje Wiener, Hongying Wang, and Dvora Yanow.

Earlier versions of some of our arguments appeared in two previous co-authored publications: "Le Constructivisme dans la Théorie des Relations Internationales" [Constructivism in International Relations Theory], *Critique Internationale* 1 (2): 51–62 (published by Presses de Sciences Po) and "Translating Terminologies," in "The Forum: Moving Beyond the Agent-Structure Debate in International Relations," *International Studies Review* 8 (2): 356–362 (published by Blackwell Publishing and the International Studies Association).

# STRATEGIES FOR RESEARCH
## in Constructivist International Relations

# Chapter One

# Constructivism

The end of the Cold War shattered stable antagonisms and alliances, both in the practice of world politics and in the study of International Relations (IR). This destabilization widened the political and intellectual spaces—and increased the need—for scholars to ask questions about the cultural bases of conflict, alternative conceptions of national identity, the ethics of intervention, and many other issues. Many practitioners and researchers now accept the "constructivist" view that individuals and groups are not only shaped by their world but can also change it. People can—but do not always —set into motion new normative, cultural, economic, social, or political practices that alter conventional wisdoms and standard operating procedures.

The IR community's embrace of constructivism built upon the work of pioneering theorists who contested the central premises of dominant structuralist (Realist, Liberal, and Marxist) frameworks by insisting that interpretations produce social reality (Ashley 1984; Wendt 1987; Wendt and Duvall 1989; Kratochwil 1989; Onuf 1989). Constructivists stress that both structural continuities and processes of change are based on agency. Agency, in turn, is influenced by social, spatial, and historical context. Rather than granting ontological priority to either structure or agency, constructivists view both as "mutually constituted." Thus they also reject the individualism inherent in rationalist theories of choice, which take for granted the nature of actors' interests and identities. The constructivist agenda in IR has flourished due to sustained attention to the implications of these ontological and epistemological concerns.

Taking seriously the principle that social reality is produced through meaningful action, however, leads to its own research challenges. Perhaps due to a (misplaced) tendency to equate all work on "ideas" with constructivism, researchers often seem unsure what concepts and methods to apply. Our students and colleagues inevitably ask: How do I do constructivist research? What kinds of processes are constitutive? Where do I find appropriate evidence? We sympathize with this uncertainty, because we asked the same questions in our own early work. Back in the late 1980s, few models demonstrated how to apply meta-theoretical insights to the policy changes that interested us, specifically, global responses to racial discrimination (Klotz 1995) and the roles of peace movements (Lynch 1999a).

This book is designed for those who want to apply constructivist insights but seek guidance on the "how," "what," and "where" questions of empirical research. By using examples from the now numerous empirical studies that draw upon sociology, jurisprudence, philosophy, linguistics, anthropology, cultural studies, history, and other approaches, we draw attention to diverse, and sometimes implicit, methodological issues. We emphasize concepts and tools that help researchers to examine, interpret, and analyze both continuity and change. Our aim is to glean strategies for designing research projects rather than to advocate any single model or set of methods. While we presume that our readers have been introduced to the meta-theoretical debates (e.g., Ruggie 1998; Guzzini 2000; Adler 2002; Ba and Hoffmann 2003), we also include an appendix of annotated Suggested Readings for those who wish to explore constructivism's interdisciplinary heritage.

While the constructivist label has allowed our work to find a home in the field, we also acknowledge the inherent problem of referring to all these voices as a single "-ism." The term means many things to its various practitioners, despite the common focus on capturing processes of mutual constitution. Even the two of us define concepts and use tools differently, while researching similar questions about transnational social movements and international norms. Because boundaries remain inherently fluid, we remain especially wary of attempts to separate "mainstream" causal analysis from "radical" postmodernism (cf., Checkel 1997; Campbell 1998a; Hopf 1998). Such divisions overlook commonalities, leading researchers to miss opportunities to learn from each other. Therefore, we embrace boundary-crossing efforts, such as critical social theory and feminism (Price and Reus-Smit 1998; Ackerly and True 2001; Locher and Prügl 2001), along with many other interjections. Indeed, we discuss some scholars who may avoid using the label themselves if, in our view, their approaches explore processes of mutual constitution.

One way to delve more productively into these differences is to contrast the methodological implications of alternative social, rationalist, materialist, and psychological ontologies rather than engage in the disciplinary war of paradigms. We find that perpetuating divisions between Realists, Liberals, and Marxists papers over commonalities across rival schools, downplays intra-paradigm differences, and does little to illuminate the constructivist ontological challenge to all three perspectives. In order to improve disciplinary understandings of nuclear proliferation, divisions between rich and poor, the nature of security, and the role of transnational actors, among other shared concerns, researchers should grapple head-on with often-vociferous disagreements rather than finding shelter in intellectual camps. Indeed, labels such as "liberal constructivist" and "realist constructivist" are gaining popularity, offering the potential for creative synergies (Risse 2002; Barkin 2003; Forum 2004).

Bridge-building requires openness to the terminologies used in alternative schools of thought. Sophisticated language expresses nuances but also risks turning into jargon. Not everyone, for example, shares our preference for the term "intersubjectivity" (which we discuss in the next section). Our goal is to demonstrate the benefits of tacking back and forth between terminologies without overly simplifying subtle theoretical points. We demonstrate how similar research problems can be explored with various methods and draw out some of the stakes involved in framing questions in different ways. Productive tensions exist that we cannot resolve here; we acknowledge these openly and offer some strategies for addressing them.

To keep the volume concise and accessible, we avoid extensive citations and often synthesize multiple works into general claims. References to "some" or "other" constructivists represent our own (contestable) readings of the growing literature. Despite our intention to be inclusive and balanced, some people and topics inevitably get more attention than others. Indeed, no one could present a comprehensive survey. Often we select examples that we have used effectively in our own teaching. Other studies may not be as explicit in their choice of methods, or they might cover a different topic than those we have chosen to highlight. Because our aim is to demonstrate the utility of methods for capturing specific constructivist insights, we primarily emphasize contributions rather than any shortcomings. We leave it to other researchers to extend these applications and demarcate their limitations.

The remainder of this chapter summarizes key themes in constructivist research and clarifies terminology used in the subsequent chapters. We set out a core vocabulary and conceptual terrain in four steps: ontology, epistemology, methodology, and validity. The next two chapters highlight six methods used in empirical work, concentrating on issues of structure in Chapter 2 and agency in Chapter 3. In such a survey, we cannot provide a thorough account of the origins and potential uses of every technique. Instead, we highlight how each tool can capture some key aspects of mutual constitution. (Citations along the way and the appendix of Suggested Readings provide references to more detailed guidelines for using these tools.) In order to assess the stakes involved in choosing between these methodologies, we then concentrate on two core issues of research design: defining concepts in Chapter 4, and selecting cases in Chapter 5. From this cumulative assessment across chapters, readers should be able to identify the particular techniques most appropriate for their own research questions.

## Ontology: How Do Researchers Conceptualize What They Study?

People live within and interact through overlapping social (ethnic, national, ideological, gendered, cultural, religious, and other) groupings, including states. Such collectivities, including leaders within them, act in ways that create, perpetuate, and alter the environments in which they live. If people did not reinforce dominant meanings, sometimes expressed as historical "facts" or unavoidable "reality," structures would not exist. The use of language about ethnicity, for instance, tends to encourage the pursuit of collective goals based on race or religion while often devaluing those that stress gender or class distinctions. But religious beliefs and the boundaries of membership within ethnic groups do evolve over time. And neither gender nor class is a static category. These instabilities and ambiguities offer opportunities to redefine routine practices. For instance, women, embracing multiple identities, might mobilize for equal rights within a religious or ethnic group and, as an unintended consequence, improve their economic condition.

Constructivists characterize this interactive relationship between what people do and how societies shape their actions as the "mutual constitution" of structures and agents. Yet the simultaneity of this interaction creates difficulties for capturing both the self-reinforcing nature of structures and the ways in which people sometimes overturn social order. People consciously *and* unintentionally replicate *and* challenge institutionalized routines and prevailing assumptions. We do not aspire to resolve long-standing philosophical issues at the heart of this "agent structure debate" (Forum 2006). Rather, we seek strategies for untangling various mechanisms of mutual constitution in empirical research. The first step in tackling this challenge, in our view, is to recognize that constructivist ontology relies on three components: intersubjectivity, context, and power. We elaborate on the significance of each of these core concepts before turning to their epistemological implications.

### Intersubjectivity

In the constructivist view, intersubjective understandings comprise structures and agents. These norms, rules, meanings, languages, cultures, and ideologies are social phenomena that create identities and guide actions. More than one person needs to accept these social phenomena in order for them to exist, and people define themselves in reference to them. Intersubjective understandings are more than aggregated beliefs of individuals. Money, for example, requires shared acceptance that tokens can be exchanged for goods, which in turn requires general agreement among buyers and sellers on what coins, papers, or entries into a computer spreadsheet are worth. Corporations, in turn, would not exist without the concept of profit, defined in terms of money. Domestic and international laws, such as trade regimes, also depend on such a monetary system. Rules and norms establish the habitual practices and procedures that we know as capitalism. The world economy shapes how people see the world, the goals they wish to accomplish, and the actions they take.

Particular meanings become stable over time, creating social orders that constructivists call structures or institutions. Rules and norms set expectations about how the world works, what types of behavior are legitimate, and which interests or identities are possible. World leaders generally acknowledge norms of warfare, for example, even when they dispute their application to specific situations. In denying the applicability of the prohibition against aggressive war, for instance, Iraq argued that its 1990 invasion of Kuwait sought to overturn a historical injustice by former imperial powers. That an international coalition intervened illustrates the potential pitfalls of unpersuasive justifications. When the United States framed its 2003 attack on Iraq as a case of pre-emptive self-defense rather than aggression, the United Nations did not accept this interpretation. The United States, consequently, was unable to build a coalition comparable to that of the first Persian Gulf war. Its officials subsequently sought to frame its invasion of Iraq in the context of a broader war on terrorism, an interpretation that was also unpersuasive for most countries.

Meanings, such as a particular definition of terrorism, provide the basis for social orders, but they can also be contested. Though some practices inevitably dominate others at particular moments, even the most stable structures evolve. Indeed, as we discuss further below, researchers debate which labels to use for intersubjective phenomena in part because some terms, such as "norms," emphasize stability and imply broad acceptance whereas others, such as "representations," privilege potentially more fluid depictions and suggest greater contestation. For the moment, we set aside those debates and use all of these terms somewhat interchangeably, in order to concentrate on the implications of this ontological focus on contested and evolving meanings.

## Context

Because intersubjective understandings vary across regions, over time, and within hierarchies, constructivists situate research questions within spatial, historical, and social contexts. To understand how shifts in meaning affect people living in particular regions and eras—and to gauge the potential for people to transform standard practices—researchers need to avoid reified, essentialized, or static notions of culture which preclude the possibility of change. For example, one might characterize contemporary capitalism as an ideology that includes a concept of money based on exchange rates, rather than gold, and the legitimacy of wage labor, rather than indentured servitude. Yet capitalism, like any ideology, manifests itself differently over time. Not surprisingly, therefore, the International Monetary Fund and the World Bank propagated certain fiscal, monetary, trade, and welfare policies in the second half of the twentieth century that are now seen as less legitimate. Accepted desires and behaviors in one period or society may be derided at other times, in other places, or by people in other social settings. For instance, the General Agreement of Tariffs and Trade morphed into the World Trade Organization, an idea shot down as too radical half a century earlier when proposed in the form of an International Trade Organization.

These changes need not follow a linear or teleological path. Prevailing practices, such as the current global market system and liberal financial institutions, spread unevenly across time and space. So do challenges to them, such as protests against globalization. The activities of contemporary environmental, human rights, and feminist groups may alter practices or institutions in some places but their efforts may be limited or blocked elsewhere. As a result, wage labor prevails around the globe, but not all forms of slavery or servitude have been eliminated. Similarly, protestant princes undermined the influence of the Catholic Church but the Vatican continues to play a significant role in many regions of the world, and anti-colonial movements gained formal independence for national territories but did not necessarily achieve economic or political autonomy.

In keeping with constructivism's emphasis on intersubjectivity, evaluations of the successes or failures of these groups take into account whether people altered their thinking about their own place in the world, as well as the legitimate role of other actors, such as governments and corporations. These assessments, furthermore, will be informed by the researchers' own normative views, because analysts live in a particular spatial location and social setting within the contemporary liberal capitalist order. This relationship between researcher and interpretation underscores the discursive rather than material conception of power that underpins the analysis of meaning within particular spatial, historical, and social contexts.

## *Power*

Because multiple meanings coexist, often in tension with one another, constructivists ask how and why certain practices prevail in particular contexts. Dominant intersubjective understandings, such as those that defined American and Soviet as enemies rather than allies during the Cold War, are characterized as powerful because they constitute people's identities and interests, as well as frame interpretations of behavior. The habitual actions that emanate from these interpretations are often referred to as "practices," and the combination of language and techniques employed to maintain them as "discourses." Despite the emphasis on dominant understandings, this is not simply a substitution of language for material resources such as nuclear warheads. All people exercise some degree of power, because their practices either reinforce or undermine meanings. For example, European peace and human rights groups contributed to the end of the Cold War by articulating continent-wide interests rather than reiterating enmity and reinscribing spheres of influence. Mikhail Gorbachev took up and modified these new articulations in ways that resulted in the unintended (for him) break-up of the Soviet Union.

Since power operates through relationships rather than possession of capabilities, constructivists analyze processes and interactions. One might view the Cold War as an ideological conflict between capitalism and communism, which created a bipolar system through escalating military spending. Arms control treaties, such as the US-Soviet anti-ballistic missile accords and, later, the global land mines ban, altered how actors calculated the desirability of certain weapons systems, regardless of any military efficacy. The resulting asymmetrical distribution of military capabilities also produces incentives and justifications for contemporary non-state actors to use weapons and tactics that differ from those of disgruntled groups in previous eras. Actors define who they are and what they want with reference to the dominant rules and ideologies of their time.

This conception of the exercise of power as the ability to reconstruct discourses and shape practices offers researchers a framework for assessing how meanings condition identities and actions, why some dominate others, and when these patterns shift. It also broadens the scope of our analysis beyond behavior to include how people justify their actions. Granting the role of language such a fundamental place in the analysis raises epistemological issues about how to study this intersubjective reality.

## Epistemology: How Do Researchers Know What They Know?

In reviewing a broad range of empirical studies, we found more overlap between epistemological positions than current debates led us to expect. Too much intellectual energy, in our view, goes into creating and maintaining boundaries between stylized camps. Caricatures of ahistoricism or relativism easily lead constructivists to lose sight of subtler issues. As an alternative, we offer the less-rigid notion of a spectrum from positivist-leaning to post-positivist positions. This heuristic resists the elevation of one philosophy of social science over another. Rather than clustering at the poles, most researchers make knowledge claims that fall at different points along a wide range. Therefore, we use the term "empiri-cal" loosely to refer to diverse types of evidence, and are not tied to the correspondence theory of truth that is associated with an "empiricist" epistemology.

Abiding differences along this spectrum do hold significance for empirical analyses. Even though constructivists share the same basic ontological starting point of mutual constitution, not all re-searchers give the same weight to structure or agency. And all talk about interpretation but use language in innumerable ways. Some offer causal explanations, while others map discourses. Shifting attention away from epistemological proclamations toward the empirical analysis of mutual constitution requires untangling two issues that define positions along our spectrum: interpretation and causality. We ask how far interpretation goes in making general inferences to get a clearer picture of the way these epistemological positions overlap or diverge.

## Interpretation

The ontological premise that structure and agency are mutually constituted through intersubjective understandings leads to the re-jection of the existence of objective facts distinct from the concepts that give them meaning (see Suggested Readings). All researchers engage in interpretation, both in collecting evidence and when making choices about what questions to research. But constructiv-ists disagree about how far interpretation must go. For example, some take for granted the dominance of a liberal understanding of human rights norms in assessing democratization, while others probe the roots of such ideological hegemony. The researcher's own acceptance or criticism of liberal values will influence—at least to some extent—both the general research agenda and the resulting analysis. Comparing any other country's policies with South Afri-can apartheid communicates moral judgment, for instance, while using South Africa as a model of democratization downplays issues of economic inequality.

We place researchers toward the positivist end of our epistemo-logical spectrum if they study reality in terms of stable meanings, such as human rights norms, and believe that neither prevalent ideologies nor the researcher's own judgments have a significant impact on the reliability of the resulting analysis. Norms, as "social facts," exist "by virtue of all the relevant actors agreeing that they exist" (Ruggie 1998: 12; also see Suggested Readings). Codified norms, for instance, define what counts as a rights violation, leading analysts to assess the strength of those norms. In this view, theoretical frameworks, unaffected by hermeneutic issues, guide conclusions about the empirical evidence. Analysts do not need to examine whether the norms at issue cohere or "fit" best with, say, liberal notions of individual human rights (instead of, perhaps, post-colonial conceptualizations). Because scholars describe and explain characteristics, patterns, and relationships between such norms, debates center on rival theoretical frameworks and core concepts.

Those on the post-positivist side of the spectrum, in contrast, do not attribute essential properties to social facts. Dominant actors can agree on what constitutes human rights at a particular point in time, but these meanings are contested (often by marginalized actors) and inherently unstable. These researchers prefer terminology such as "representations" to connote this greater fluidity. Scholars inevitably work in a hermeneutical circle of ever-deeper and more implicit interpretations, where their own generalizations, among other issues, become complicit in prevalent interpretive frameworks. Knowledge—as truth claims rather than objective historical facts—thus becomes intertwined with power, resulting in "regimes of truth" that perpetuate particular (unequal) relationships. Liberal individualism underlies the so-called Western notion of human rights, Realism provides the dominant meta-narrative for analyzing Cold War foreign policies, and Marxism serves that role for many critics of globalization. Whereas the positivist sees social facts as relatively unproblematic, the post-positivist sees them as in need of ideological excavation.

As authors, the two of us gravitate towards opposite poles on this spectrum. But unlike those who insist on the primacy of one or the other epistemology, we treat the (in-)stability of intersubjective understandings as an empirical question. We agree that particular meanings can sometimes be treated as stable social facts, even though this assumption may be problematic at other times. For example, any researcher might reach the empirical conclusion that international law codifies liberal human rights norms, which act as relatively stable social facts in transnational interactions. Researchers can also examine challenges to these norms. They might differ on empirical and normative grounds whether such contestation should be treated as significant or insignificant, positive or negative. Post-positivists accept enough stability in meanings to employ language, describe discourses, and theorize power. Positivist-leaning constructivists are concerned with fluidity, although they refer to "change" rather than "contestation." Consequently, we do not judge scholarship based on the terminology that the researcher uses. Rather, we assess it according to the insights it provides about the relationships between structures and agents.

## *Causality*

Constructivists on the positivist end of the spectrum seek to explain social phenomena in general terms. Although they reject any aspiration to identify "laws" of behavior, they do place high priority on the applicability of their explanations across a wide empirical range. Post-positivists, in turn, remain more comfortable with complexity and context-specific claims. They usually seek a (relatively) comprehensive understanding of one or a few cases, though they may draw "lessons" from them. This greater stress on uniqueness of experience is often characterized in epistemological debates as the search for understanding, an approach associated with humanistic disciplines such as history and anthropology (in contrast to economics or sociology). But this dichotomy between explanation and understanding relies on overdrawn distinctions between science and the humanities. In the past fifty years, anthropology, history, economics, and sociology, as well as political science and IR, have all had their proponents and critics of science. In the midst of these debates, constructivists offer complex, multi-causal, contextualized explanations; to do otherwise would contradict basic ontological assumptions. Differences hinge on what these claims are about, not whether claims are being made.

The main dividing line among constructivists is the putative distinction between constitutive and causal claims. Yet few clear markers differentiate the two, because the language of "causality" is quite fluid. Separating constitutive "how possible" questions from causal "why" questions mirrors the problematic distinction between explanation and understanding. Yes, causal studies do tend to speak in terms of explaining behavior, while studies of meaning talk about understanding the conditions for action. Certainly the terms are not interchangeable, but in practice there is considerable overlap. Those who say they explain behavior also interpret meaning, and those who focus on understanding language also explain action to some degree. Alternatively, separating properties from actions as a way to distinguish constitutive and causal questions understates the extent to which actions define those very properties; "how possible" questions quietly shift to "what" questions. Categorization answers "what" questions, but typology is also a key component of explanation, leaving no clear divide between "what" or "how" or "why" questions. Constructivists should not, therefore, preclude the possibility of causal answers to constitutive questions, or vice versa.

Refocusing on the ontology of mutual constitution leads us to rethink these issues in terms of structure and agency. Structural approaches, be they ideational or material, focus on the possibilities for, and constraints upon, action. The notion of conditional causality captures the effects of structure. Given a particular set of social, historical, and/or spatial conditions, people are likely to act in predictable ways (in positivist terminology) or reproduce dominant practices (in post-positivist terminology). Such analyses allow for context-dependent generalizations about behavior and language. Answers to "how possible" questions describe the conditions that comprise these contexts, regardless of whether analysts label them variables. Any claims about the strength of these preconditions rely on correlational logic until researchers propose mechanisms to explain why certain conditions lead to particular actions. Such attention to mechanisms emphasizes that processes shape the relationships between structures and agents.

Clarifying the issue of causality reveals how much alternative constructivist claims about people's behavior are ontologically rather than epistemologically driven. People might act in particular ways because they have been conditioned to do so by language, which precludes alternative understandings of the world. Alternatively, they may consciously calculate the social and material benefits in particular situations. Those who assume instrumental rationality will examine the ranking of goals, while those who presume that action results from habit might describe the rules that define social roles. Rather than making assumptions about the basis for action, researchers should probe these as competing explanations.

We reserve for later in the chapter how to assess the validity of such alternatives. For the moment, we simply underscore that language, meaning, symbols, culture, discourse—all the intersubjective phenomena at the heart of the constructivist ontology—remain vital components of "why" analysis, because constructivists presume human intentionality. People's reasoning processes, both through instrumental calculations and moral arguments, remain empirical issues to be investigated with a range of appropriate methodological tools.

## Methodology: How Do Researchers Select Their Tools?

While we have thus far made a case that epistemological differences in practice lack clear boundaries, these distinctions do persist across the social sciences. The behavioral revolution of the 1950s did not stop anthropologists from using ethnography in an effort to understand societies, and sociologists tend to make causal arguments even after their linguistic turn in the 1980s. Constructivist researchers frequently replicate these disciplinary traditions. Rather than accepting any stark division between techniques as inherently suitable for analyzing meaning or behavior, we consider the definition of core concepts as the starting point for exploring methodological choices. Only then can analysts assess which tools are best suited to capturing the processes of mutual constitution that are at the heart of the constructivist approach.

To illustrate the importance of conceptualization as a key element of methodology, we compare how two groups of constructivists have used variants of discourse analysis to develop cross-disciplinary perspectives on "strategic culture." The volume on the avowedly positivist end of the epistemological spectrum, *The Culture of National Security: Norms and Identity in World Politics* (Katzenstein, ed. 1996), draws on sociological concepts associated with hypotheses and generalization. In contrast, *Cultures of Insecurity: States, Communities, and the Production of Danger* (Weldes et al, eds. 1999) draws explicitly on anthropological insights.

## Concepts

Constructivists see "security" as a relationship historically conditioned by culture rather than an objective characteristic determined by the distribution of military capabilities. Consequently, we favor methodologies that acknowledge contingency and context. Indeed, contributors to both *The Culture of National Security* and *Cultures of Insecurity* acknowledge the need for some type of interpretation. Across both volumes, many of the authors also select single or comparative cases with a historical perspective, seeking more complete stories based on a wider range of documentation or a reinterpretation of previous studies. However, these common research concerns get articulated through different theoretical vocabularies.

The titles alone signal each group's epistemological position. On the positivist side, "culture" and "identity," both in the singular, and "norms" imply that meanings can be stable and knowable independent of the interpretive biases. Culture and identity, therefore, are isolated from other characteristics of social life, to be treated as variables that explain the choices states make in military policy, offering a basis for comparisons across cases. Many contributors focus on particular norms either prohibiting or encouraging strategic behavior, including patterns of conventional weapons proliferation, taboos on the use of chemical and nuclear weapons, and evolving practices of humanitarian intervention. Because communities of people often articulate shared expectations, in the process endowing them with normative force, scholars can use texts, including official (national or international) documents, to demonstrate general patterns of state compliance. These patterns can substantiate claims that norms influence behavior. Others remain skeptical of arguments relying solely on public pro- nouncements and correlated patterns of behavior; they want more insight into policy-making processes, leading to greater emphasis on interviews, among other tools.

But once researchers allow for cultural change over time or space, the door opens to contending worldviews—no single or coherent culture necessarily predominates. The post-positivist vocabulary of "production" and multiple "cultures" therefore suggests fluidity, malleability, contestation, and contingency in social understandings, including dominant frameworks and the researcher's own assumptions. Instead of identifying a stable military culture that predictably influences policies, these scholars start by assuming that such a culture is never fixed and takes a fair amount of work to perpetuate. Rather than being the outcome to be analyzed, policies signify particular notions of security. In this vein, many contributors to *Cultures of Insecurity* focus on how discourses produce dominant representations of threat in areas diverse as Asia, North America, the Middle East, cyberspace, and academia. Understanding patterns of domination within these con- texts explicitly and profoundly challenges the equation of military capabilities with power.

### Tools

Do these differences between sociological and anthropological vari- ants of constructivism create an unbridgeable methodological di- vide? We think not. Evidence from policy discourse, such as public pronouncements, secret policy debates, and interviews, can support both positivist and post-positivist formulations of security studies. For instance, both critical theorists and problem-solvers who focus on social movements frequently rely on non-governmental archival materials and ethnographic techniques. Yet, as in the elite-oriented studies, these scholars can reach different conclusions about the nature of power and policy-making processes based on the same evidence. Concepts, rather than the tools for collecting evidence, lead to alternative interpretations.

Since any interpreter benefits from the widest array of evidence, we recommend that scholars develop proficiency in all techniques of "discourse analysis," not simply those associated with a particular disciplinary approach. For example, studying the language of rules or norms starts with texts to show the existence (and possibly dominance) of particular intersubjective understandings. Relevant primary sources include archives of governments, intergovernmental organizations, and non-governmental organizations, letters and memoirs of key individuals, press reports, and interviews, supplemented and contextualized through secondary sources. Treaties, conventions, negotiations, and procedures also manifest actions, such as promising or threatening. Researchers should not overlook nonlinguistic dimensions of discourse. Practices, such as how people wear clothing, convey meanings that need to be interpreted through non-textual evidence. Uniforms decorated with medals and ribbons, for instance, designate individual places and social hierarchies within the military.

Not surprisingly, a wide range of tools has been developed across the social sciences and humanities to grapple with such diverse forms of evidence. Discourse analysis therefore broadly denotes methodologies that capture the creation of meanings and accompanying processes of communication. As long as words and activities are put into context, researchers can categorize, code, or count their use through many different—qualitative and quantitative—techniques. To make assessments of the relative importance of particular meanings requires some sort of comparison, across time or space, and a baseline or metric for gauging change. But many types of implicit and explicit comparisons can be used.

Ultimately, methodological choices will be influenced by the researcher's own commitments, a factor that we cannot filter. Our readers should remember that our own philosophical and ethical worldviews—including our interest in social movements—influence the themes that we highlight in our assessments of research designs. For that, we make no apologies. But such influence does raise the question of whether analysts can apply general standards in evaluating scholarship. We turn, therefore, to the issue of validity.

## Validity: How Do Researchers Evaluate Their Interpretations?

While none of us claim to offer the correct interpretation of an objective reality, constructivists agree that not every interpretation is equally supportable. Therefore scholars need some basis for selecting one analysis as somehow more reasonable or plausible than another. To a surprising degree, constructivists accept that empirical inconsistencies undermine the persuasiveness of interpretations, regardless of whether they are part of simplifying models meant to be applied across a range of cases or an analysis of multiple interactions in one particular instance. Researchers strive to gather a variety of source materials in order to check one against another ("triangulate"), rather than selecting only those that confirm prior expectations ("bias"). Familiarity with the strengths and weaknesses of a range of methodological tools enables better assessments.

Yet even this shared standard is value-laden. The selection of measures against which to gauge "accuracy" will reflect meta-theoretical assumptions that underpin the definition of core concepts (Adcock and Collier 2001; Rudolph 2005; Lynch 2006). Even more fundamentally, what counts as a coherent argument depends on many implicit social assumptions, including cosmologies about human nature and non-human agency. Some concepts also resonate better with people in particular social or historical situations, influencing what they accept as logical. What to do with these knowledge claims, such as whether to challenge the ethical implications of particular definitions of core concepts or respond to policy problems, is another question.

### Generalization

Constructivists remain skeptical of strong generalizations and favor context-specific analysis, regardless of whether one speaks in the vocabulary of social science or critical theory. Within a social ontology, knowledge cannot be about accurate measures of objective facts. Yet, in one way or another, scholars do make truth claims. This leads analysts to wrestle with tensions between generalization and detail, because we cannot achieve both simultaneously to the same degree. A simplified theoretical framework produces a more stylized empirical analysis, while total immersion into evidence makes no sense without some sort of theoretical framework. Interpretation requires at least some key concepts to guide the selection of relevant information. In turn, those concepts result from researchers trying to understand, and act within, their socially constructed world. Theory and evidence thus inform each other. The more credible claim combines the insights of studies that rely on generalization with others that stress detail.

These judgments depend on the researcher's question and analytical goal, not the number of cases. Some scholars delve into a single case, using either change over time or perhaps theories as counterfactual foils upon which to build hypothetical alternatives. Others prefer to cover, or at least sample, as many cases as possible, often leading to the use of quantitative approaches (if they avoid overly rigid measures). There are many permutations and combinations of cases, such as paired comparisons within a broader study. Some selections highlight similarities across cases, others variation between them. These comparisons enable scholars to probe the coherence of alternative interpretations. A combination of logic and consistency in the use of evidence thus distinguishes "better" scholarship.

### Standards

The very nature of the academic system, including grades and peer review of publications, means that scholars constantly judge the quality of research. Professors assign "good" work for course readings and urge students to emulate the "best" research. Such praise necessarily relies on comparison. Implicitly and explicitly, researchers evaluate descriptions and causal claims relative to competing descriptions and claims. An explanation might be logically more coherent if its core conceptual starting point was more clearly defined, for instance. And a particular historical interpretation might be more convincing if the author had been able to incorporate a broader range of archival materials, some of which appear to contradict the main argument. Acceptance of these standards regulates our profession.

Sometimes, however, contrasting explanations lead us to recognize important differences between what, how, or why questions. For example, one might ask whether constructivist studies of security differ significantly from a traditional bureaucratic approach to foreign policy. One response is found in those contributions to *The Culture of National Security* that describe strategic cultures in countries such as China, France, Germany, and Japan. By rejecting the idea of a singular national culture that remains unchanged over time, and instead locating significant influence in the practices of military and strategic decision-making, these studies question many conventional approaches to bureaucracies, which tend to take broader societal and historical contexts for granted. Those in *Cultures of Insecurity*, in turn, reconsider the significance of the policies that these bureaucracies produce. States, or their leaders, may seek to reinforce identities, for instance, rather than aim to achieve instrumental goals. Researchers might ask, then, when the cultural context of a bureaucracy matters, and why leaders sometimes value identity-affirmation over strategic or economic benefits.

## Book Overview

We hope that greater awareness that constructivists of all epistemological stripes agree on basic standards of scholarship will foster synergies across methodological proclivities. In this light, we challenge the prevailing epistemological camps to disarm in order to achieve the common goal of understanding the exercise of power and its consequences. Regardless of whether one looks at "norms" or "representations," constructivists seek to understand how certain meanings get taken for granted or dominate while others remain unspoken or marginalized. Researchers also try to discern the consequences of prevailing assumptions and the reasons why some get challenged but others do not.

To assess the stakes involved in selecting among different methodologies, we have organized the book around four key constructivist concepts: structure, agency, identities, and interests. This format enables us to concentrate on studies that ask similar questions but seek answers in different ways. Within each chapter, we outline various approaches, focusing on the strengths of each and some trade-offs between them, along with a few caveats about potential difficulties in their application. Across chapters, we point out key tasks for research design, such as distinguishing between process and outcome, combining levels of analysis, selecting comparisons, and differentiating constitutive from instrumental dynamics. Our goal is to highlight complementarities, not to propose one correct way to pursue research.

We start by sampling the diverse tools available. In Chapter 2, we introduce macro-historical comparison, genealogy, and participant-observation as techniques for analyzing institutionalization and structural change. Then we turn to approaches oriented toward understanding how people act within those structures. Chapter 3 covers narrative, framing, and ethnography. Of course, none of these six tools alone suffice, because constructivism seeks to understand mutual constitution of agents and structures. Therefore, we juxtapose some of these tools in Chapters 4 and 5. To explore the constitution of identities, we contrast genealogy with narrative and framing with ethnography. We then turn to static comparison versus process-tracing in the constitution of interests. Since we optimistically stress the potential for synergies throughout these chapters, our concluding reflections in Chapter 6 confront some of the persistent barriers to deeper dialogue among constructivists.

# Chapter Two

# Structure

For constructivists, stable meanings form structures. Discursive repetition of Cold War era rivalries, for instance, stabilized identities within institutions, such as NATO. Most often these structures change at the margins, but occasionally they shift quite dramatically. The inherently contestable relationship between contending meanings opens up possibilities for innovation and reform, such as nuclear disarmament or the destruction of the Berlin Wall. The stability of nuclear deterrence during the revolutions in Eastern Europe illustrates that people can concurrently replicate and challenge prevailing social assumptions. New human rights norms, economic ideologies, and languages of enmity or friendship may redefine the purposes of military or economic capabilities, producing a system-wide shift that transforms relationships, in the Cold War case, between the United States, the Soviet Union, Europe, and the rest of the world. Alterations in some institutions, such as in the legitimacy of particular domestic regimes in Europe, can denote a system change without concomitant transformation in other structures, such as norms of sovereignty which ensure the continued existence of these countries.

With meanings flowing between people and across borders, power relies on the dominance of particular shared understandings, rather than simply control over military technology or capital investment. Following the demise of communism in Europe, for instance, previously inconceivable relationships became possible. To analyze this evolution of the international system, constructivists trace people's perspectives on, say, nuclear weapons or factories. By exploring the contexts within which meanings form structures, constructivists examine when, how and why particular practices become relatively fixed while others remain fluid. Through rules of behavior, such as practices of diplomacy, institutions fulfill functions that reflect mutual understandings about providing order, stabilizing actors' expectations, and managing power relationships. When institutions persist, at least in the eyes of observers, structures (the clusters of rules and stable meanings that result from institutional practices) gain causal and normative force, because people act based upon (or in reaction against) these patterns and rules (Wendt and Duvall 1989; Onuf 1998; Wendt 1999).

As the term structure increasingly encompasses almost all types of social order, including global social systems, issue-specific international regimes, and formal organizations, some constructivists advocate dropping it from our vocabulary. Others go even further, arguing that it implies too great a degree of stability in meanings. In contrast, we remain comfortable with the term but distinguish alternative forms of structure across levels of analysis and degrees of aggregation: meanings stabilize into rules; sets of rules constitute institutions; clusters of institutions constitute structures, which in turn are the building blocks of systems. Rather than replaying arguments comparing materialist, rationalist, and constructivist frameworks (Hasenclever et al. 1997; Katzenstein et al. 1998), we examine ways in which the selection of alternative forms of discourse affects how researchers frame substantive questions and choose among interpretive methods. Exploring manifestations of structure at three levels of analysis, we review how scholars use macro-historical comparison, genealogy, and participant observation.

## Macro-History

Some of the earliest empirical constructivist work in IR built on historiography to show that states have not always been the primary "units" of the international system, nor have these units performed the same functions across time (Ruggie 1983). The medieval world system, for example, was one of overlapping sovereignties among heterogeneous units, with the Catholic Church heading a hierarchical order. This interpretation challenges the basic tenets of Realism, which claim that modern states, and state-like units in all earlier periods, operate in a self-help system devoid of any over-arching authority. To demonstrate such sweeping historical variation requires "huge" comparisons that tease out significant components of "big" structures and that identify "large" processes underlying these shifts between ancient, medieval, and modern systems (Tilly 1984; Mahoney and Rueschemeyer, eds. 2003). With the characterizations of ancient and medieval systems as comparative points of reference, we can then probe the nature of the contemporary international system more deeply.

## Comparisons

Constructivists debate the baseline for comparing temporal periods and the relevant units of an international system. For example, Reus-Smit (1999) challenges the commonplace reference to *The Peloponnesian War* as evidence of an enduring anarchy from ancient Greece to the present. Instead, he argues that Thucydides detailed how the Greeks employed moral reasoning and rhetoric in the application of conflict resolution norms. City-states valued arbitration as a way of mediating disputes, thus creating a "fundamental institution" that structured relations among them. His analysis emphasizes the links between political units, social practices that mediate relations between those units, and notions of legitimacy embedded in these practices.

Concepts such as moral authority and legitimacy provide the basis for a periodization that questions the seventeenth century as the turning point of the "modern" era. By probing in more detail the differences between the Italian city-states, the absolutist states and the modern order, Reus-Smit asserts that the multilateral and sovereign practices of the early nineteenth century differed substantially from those of the seventeenth. His emphasis on the decline of Athenian moral authority as a critical factor in shifting the balance of power among Greek city-states, rather than the distribution of military capabilities, leads to a different view of historical eras.

Alternative conceptualizations of international law, however, lead to other periodizations. For example, Der Derian (1987) combines the Marxist concept of "alienation" with a postmodern understanding of "estrangement" to offer another reading of diplomacy, starting with the mythology of ancient civilizations through the Christian era and to the present.

The preference for one over another organizing concept reminds us that these historical debates are also shaped by the worldviews of researchers. Most studies of macro-historical change display an uncritical Europeanist focus, leading Grovogui (1996) to challenge this Western dominance. Colonialism, he stresses, demonstrates that international legal instruments institutionalize power disparities. Many legal experts agree that international law is a Western construction, but they hesitate to conclude that this limits it. Grovogui counters by tracing how international law could serve as an instrument of reform while simultaneously moderating the process of decolonization. Recognizing such complexity in the effects of institutional settings, and the interaction between actors and structures in maintaining or changing those institutions, provides us with a subtler understanding of power in the international system.

### Authoritative Practices

Looking at moral authority and legitimacy can also illuminate the constitutive processes underpinning both the stability of macro-historical structures and the sources of change. Breaking down the mechanisms at stake in changing practices enables constructivists to conceive of structures as slow-moving processes. Social practices in the medieval era, based upon ecclesiastical understandings of natural law, underpinned the Church's moral authority within Europe. Yet scholars too often treat this period as static, presenting medieval Europe as under the firm grip of the Church. In contrast, Hall (1997) argues that a number of economic and social processes destabilized the relationship between monarchs and the Church. The institution of "sacerdotal legitimacy" (the notion that monarchs were divinely sanctioned) prevailed during the ninth through eleventh centuries, producing a hierarchical structure that favored the Church. But vassals and lords, chafing at their limited power, began to amass arms.

In the face of this challenge to its ecclesiastical authority, the papacy responded by offering indulgences and transcendental promises to encourage the vassal-knights to fight for the Church outside of Europe, hence the Crusades. It also gradually institutionalized chivalry as a social order among rulers (monarchs and bishops), knights, and laborers. By channeling economic and class developments into a reconstituted "Christian warrior-class," the Church thus used its moral authority to head off, for a few centuries at least, a potentially radical challenge to its power. While the Church maintained its dominance, relationships within this overarching structure evolved as a result of the interactions between challengers and authorities.

Practices also slowly evolved over time in other periods, as Reus-Smit describes. During the Renaissance, Italian city-states began to employ oratorical diplomacy, which spread as princes and kings sent around permanent diplomatic emissaries. After the Peace of Westphalia in 1648, individual monarchs consolidated their rule by modifying existing practices as well as developing new patterns of interaction. These combined the old diplomacy of regular bilateral relations with a gradually revised definition of natural law, resulting in the divine sanction of absolutist monarchs as representatives of God within discrete geographic boundaries. When the feudal system finally gave way to the nation-state system, the institution of "sovereignty" buttressed the power of absolutist monarchs over the Church. By the nineteenth and twentieth centuries, these geographically delineated nation-states became the primary political units. Multilateral diplomacy arose when Napoleon's attempt at hegemony broke down the institutions of early modern Europe and forced diplomats to seek mechanisms to encourage peaceful (in the sense of non-disruptive) interstate relations. While the Church had used moral suasion to get vassals to participate in the Crusades, moral authority in the nation-state relies on citizenship.

Macro-level structural comparisons lend themselves to the study of incremental change in the international system. However, conceiving of structures as slow-moving processes means that comparisons across eras may explore social stability or the dynamics of large-scale social changes. But there are specific methodological approaches that are better suited towards one or the other. Reus-Smit, for instance, adopts (relatively) static snapshots of institutions across societies, which demonstrate that practices do vary. Hall, in contrast, delineates changes within one society over time, which highlight the dynamics of change, such as shifting conceptions of class or group identities. By focusing on what moves people from "point a" to "point b," longitudinal comparisons help to sort out critical mechanisms of change. But any inherent emphasis on sequencing leads to questions about determinism. If history is the culmination of a particular sequence of variables or events, institutions within societies will be difficult to alter. Comparing a particular sequence in another society can offer insights into which mechanisms matter most, and when.

### Historical Evidence

Reus-Smit and Hall, along with many others who adopt macro-historical comparisons, frequently rely on secondary sources and key texts, such as *The Peloponnesian War* or the Treaty of Westphalia. When re-reading these classics, they situate the meaning of a text in its historical and cultural context, with the help of experts in related fields (e.g., history, classics, area studies) and check against other interpretations. For example, one of the reasons why Reus-Smit disagrees so strongly with Realists in their interpretation of Thucydides is that he bases his arguments about morality and arbitration with in-depth studies of ancient Greece, rather than selecting a line or two out of the Melian Dialogue (see also Lebow 2003). Similarly, those who read Machiavelli as more complicated than a proponent of "might makes right" rely on *The Discourses* as well as *The Prince*, along with secondary sources, to demonstrate the complexity of Italian understandings of rhetoric, republicanism, and power (Walker 1993). Contextualization of meaning helps to avoid (but cannot completely preclude) the penchant for projecting contemporary concerns and concepts onto people's conceptions in earlier eras.

Studies that rely heavily on secondary sources also risk the selection of only those texts that confirm a particular historical reading (Lustick 1996). The use of archival material merits further attention, particularly since constructivist scholars often question why some documents become standard points of reference for pinpointing significant junctures. The treaties comprising the Peace of Westphalia, for example, are almost always invoked to differentiate between the medieval and modern periods. Other documentary reference points include the Rights of Man, the US Declaration of Independence, the Treaty of Berlin, the UN Charter, the Bretton Woods Agreements, George Kennan's "X" article, and the Helsinki Accords. Often the choice of such documents reflects a pre-conceived understanding of state behavior or international structures. Instead, supplementing an examination of these documents with other texts of the same period, as well as secondary sources, can expand insights into just how much treaties, charters, or agreements reflected the practices of the previous order or represent something new. Analysts can then use a combination of sources to trace the processes involved in reproducing or changing practices.

The availability of primary sources, however, puts distinctive constraints on macro-historical interpretations. An example is the study of the Peloponnesian War, where researchers are limited to Thucydides's history and archeological finds. Interviewing decision-makers and reading their autobiographies to assess the putative accuracy of Thucydides's rendition of their speeches, for instance, are simply not options. Scholars should remain sensitive to the limitations that result from far-less-than-comprehensive access to evidence. This is not a constraint unique to macro-level analysis. For instance, any archive preserves only some voices (we return to this point in Chapter 3). While one can never possess all the relevant materials for any analysis, analysts should remain attuned to this problem.

**Genealogy**

As Hall's study of the interactions between the clergy, lords, knights, vassals, and peasants illustrates, constructivists see the *potential* for change even within relatively stable structures. Since that potential often remains unrealized (Cederman 1997; Mahoney and Rueschemeyer, eds. 2003), researchers explore how actors legitimize certain practices and delegitimize others. As a counter to deterministic arguments that present inevitable stages or isolate variables to explain structural shifts, a process-oriented "genealogical" approach to history emphasizes contestation over meanings and conjunctures rather than causes. Seeking to understand power relationships within particular societies and across eras, genealogy demonstrates both continuities and changes in discourses (including both language and practices). Intimately tied to the philosophy of Nietzsche (see Suggested Readings), one of the most influential examples is Foucault's (1977) comparison of medieval and modern practices of punishment, with Der Derian's (1987) study of the discourses of diplomacy from the ancient world to the present among the first applications in IR.

While genealogy can be applied at any level of analysis, it has taken hold mainly in the study of international regimes. Conceived as patterned order based on informal rules and formal organizations in a given issue-area, the concept of an "international regime" assumes that actors (usually states, but also inter-governmental bureaucracies and non-governmental organizations) share understandings about social purpose and expected behavior in managing money, trade, security, the environment, human rights, and other aspects of global governance. A cluster of early constructivist work focused on rules and norms, both within and beyond formal organizations, such as the League of Nations, International Court of Justice, General Agreement on Tariffs and Trade (GATT), and (what is now) the European Union. By delving into the intersubjective nature of these institutions, Kratochwil and Ruggie (1986) pointed to a fundamental conceptual problem: studies of regimes generally relied on observed behavior to analyze meanings. Feminists challenged the same epistemologies and methods on the grounds that they masked the gendered practices embedded in norms that reflect a "masculine" worldview (Tickner 1992). Genealogy is one method that answers the call for interpretive methods that capture the essentially intersubjective nature of regimes.

## Contested Meanings

Much of the constructivist work on regimes focuses on the characteristics and dynamics of the liberal world economy, often building on Polanyi's (1944) analysis of the relationship between property rights, financial institutions, and social purpose in the transition to capitalism in Britain. The empirical scope is broad, ranging from comparable studies of economic transitions to capitalism in other countries, the rise and decline of the gold standard, similarities and differences between the nineteenth century British and the twentieth century U.S. dominance, colonization and decolonization, the construction and operation of international financial institutions such as the International Monetary Fund (IMF) and World Bank, and the nature of contemporary globalization. Overall, these diverse studies debate, implicitly or explicitly, the relationship between material and social power.

Constructivists push beyond the "fact" of uneven distributions of power to probe how dominance gets constituted and maintained in the face of internal tensions and potential challengers. For example, by distinguishing American *hegemony* from *American* hegemony, Ruggie (1993) emphasizes that the nature of a particular hegemon and its relationships with others, not simply its preponderant resources, has substantial implications for global order—and for policy recommendations. Governments could create regimes in particular issue-areas such as money, trade, and finance after World War II through an ensemble of formal organizations, such as the IMF, the World Bank, and GATT (now the World Trade Organization). A reaction against the Great Depression and the failed economic bilateralism of the interwar period, the new rules and norms modified the market system. This agreement on "embedded liberalism" (Ruggie 1982) as a fundamental organizing principle reflected the goal of Western countries: to promote a global market system that still permitted domestic interventions to protect employment. That the United States could forge such a consensus institutionalized its dominance within a multilateral structure.

The end of the Cold War heightened processes of marketization, cultural homogenization, and technological globalization, along with increased resistance to such hegemony. Many critique the commonplace treatment of liberal practices as value-neutral. Liberalism too often becomes a cover term for the stereotypical Enlightenment mindset which prioritizes individual rights and linear notions of "progress" (Berman 2000). Some argue that liberal practices and values are part and parcel of both a militarized Cold War system and a post-Cold War one in which the consolidation of the Euopean Union and the expansion of NATO reinforce many dimensions of Western influence. Thus Latham (1997), among others, tightly links liberal economics, capitalist ideology, and militarism. While feminists have long argued that gendered perspectives on world order constitute strategic practices (e.g., Enloe 1990, 1993), they now point to ambiguities and contradictions stemming from gendered forms of globalization (e.g., Hooper 2001). For example, True (2001) shows that new capitalist marketing techniques in the Czech Republic objectify women, but that decentralized institutions also allow for wider latitude in organizing for women's rights. Freer trade can benefit some economies and societies (or subsets of actors within them), while creating social chaos and political backlash in others.

One strand of debate turns on whether ideologies, such as liberalism, are products of an underlying material basis, or whether those values operate as a constitutive dimension of power. For example, Rupert (1995, 2000) employs a Gramscian framework (drawing on Cox 1986, 1989, 1996) to critique the ideological articulations of US hegemony and to identify pockets of resistance to it. Despite incorporating a cultural dimension to power, such a Gramscian perspective ultimately relies on a Marxist ontology of materialism which reduces ideology to epiphenomenal superstructure (in the classic Marxist terminology). Thus Rupert's (2005) efforts to incorporate race and gender *into* a more fundamental class analysis contrast with those influenced more by post-structuralism, who attribute power to all identity discourses. Doty (1996) and Muppidi (2005), for example, claim that the institutionalization of US, Western, masculine, and white privilege is premised on hierarchical distinctions created through language, such as dichotomies of order/disorder and civilized/barbarian. Some people—the orderly, civilized, powerful ones—are the subjects of global governance while others—the disorderly, uncivilized, powerless ones—remain its objects.

One way to tease out the analytical stakes of these ontological differences is through explicit comparisons of, say, the impacts of globalization. However, this type of contrast risks ignoring constitutive dynamics. If material factors are socially mediated, they become the dependent variables—we cannot then posit them as an alternative set of independent variables. Constitutive analysis of, say, interest formation, would precede materialist or rationalist explanations of interest-based behavior. Comparisons can certainly be used to grasp constitutive processes; we need to be vigilant, however, in how we select them (a point we return to in Chapter 5). In contrast, genealogy as a method focuses on evolution in the contestation over meanings, such as those that underpin liberalism and US hegemony. It maps out multiple conjunctures, rather than seeking a single, overarching, causal explanation.

## Conjunctures

Genealogy starts with an awareness of structural inequalities based on the meanings of materiality. In contrast to deterministic or teleological analyses, it avoids a neat linear view of the past by identifying the mechanisms that produce shifts in dominant discourse. As a form of process tracing, genealogies stress both the techniques of power that operate within discourses, and the "ruptures" and "disjunctures" in institutionalized practices across historical periods. For example, rather than trying to isolate social, economic, and political causes of shifts between ancient, medieval, and modern international systems, Der Derian identifies continuities and discontinuities in dominant discourses of diplomacy. Similarly, Price (1995: 86) argues that the chemical weapons "taboo" strengthened over the course of the twentieth century, through appeals to a particular interpretation of humanitarianism, despite "the rather jumbled history of violations and resurrections of the CW [chemical weapon] norm."

Genealogy follows Foucault's conception of discourse as encompassing more than language. Clothing readily denotes a person's class, religion, or gender. Other "texts," including gestures, architecture, and music, also "embody" meanings. For example, the discourse of punishment institutionalizes anonymity and debasement through prison architecture and clothing, the constriction of time and space, and prohibitions on food, exercise, and entertainment, as well as the language used to describe criminality. Similarly, evidence that torture remains rife for prisoners of war leads to questions about global discourses of punishment that include a wide range of language, images, and actions, as in the global and transnational dimensions of the privatization of policing that Laffey and Weldes (2005) explore.

In analyzing diverse manifestations of discourse, genealogy generally requires that researchers tap into a wide variety of primary and secondary sources. Foucault's genealogy of punishment, for example, moves from the design of physical objects used in medieval practices of torture and the architectural construction of the nineteenth century prison to legal and popular understandings of aberrant behavior in both eras. As a result, he required legal records, documentation of political debates, and design plans for systems of incarceration or punishment. Selecting among all the potentially significant resources, therefore, is one of the most basic challenges of applying this method. Some choices will be made based on epistemological grounds, others on practical considerations of availability and access. As with any method, these will also be influenced, implicitly or explicitly, by availability and the researcher's worldview given prevailing socio-historical context.

Like other types of historical analysis, genealogy enriches or challenges previous interpretations, rather than producing one correct, objective history. While analysts can evaluate all histories based on their logic, coherence, and thoroughness in the use of sources, genealogy in particular sensitizes academics to the ways in which dominant discourses, including scholarly interpretations, can create artificial unity by appealing to certain elements of the past over others (Milliken 1999: 243). It also draws attention to alternative voices that get ignored by traditional historical methods, which tend to inscribe the experiences of the powerful. For example,

Kinsella (2005) reveals how gender, rather than biological sex difference, differentiates combatants and civilians. Unlike traditional macro-historical comparison that seeks to explain behavioral outcomes or processes, her purpose is to understand how gendered practices constitute women as innocent bystanders to war. She identifies this constitutive role of meanings by tracing the evolution of the definition of civilian in international law, contrasting in particular the early formulation of Grotius to the later framing in the 1949 Geneva Convention.

Kinsella's genealogy raises the methodological question of whether it is possible (and if so, how) to distinguish this constitutive role of meanings from other potential functions of discourses. (We use the term "function" in the sense of "purpose," with the caveat that discourses and institutions may also have unintended consequences.) Like Doty and Muppidi, discourse for Kinsella creates (often-dichotomous) categories, such as man/woman and combatant/civilian. The distinctions between civilized and uncivilized, upon which identities are based, consequently frame judgments about actions, such as condemnation of the use of rape during wartime or the failure to deliver comparable benefits to women soldiers. Those actions created a recursive relationship that replicates the meanings upon which they are predicated, thus precluding a traditional linear, causal, analysis between independent and dependent variables.

By highlighting the ideological underpinnings and discursive manifestations of hegemony, these scholars remind us that we as researchers also work within these normative settings. Because socialization leads us to replicate practices legitimated by prevailing structures, genealogy trains us to pay more attention to the ways in which we stabilize and reproduce discourse, such as in our use of words such as sex and gender. As researchers, we necessarily participate in our social settings. Religious views, for example, will shape how we study moral authority; gender can influence our definitions of insecurity. Our own theoretical commitments and underlying conceptual assumptions lead us to examine selective aspects of history.

Academics, as scholars and teachers, thus play a significant role in the maintenance of "epistemic" power, because we produce knowledge claims and disseminate them through our writing and lecturing. Our discourses create systems of meaning which embody relations of power (Dreyfus and Rabinow 1982; Adler and Bernstein 2005). We cannot remain value-neutral, because we automatically either replicate or challenge embedded assumptions through our scholarship. Bias, therefore, can never be eliminated, though we can strive to be self-aware, in order to understand the moral and methodological implications of our choices. Whether researchers can compensate for bias is a debated point. Some argue that we can never become aware of all our implicit assumptions. Others point to the potential to retrain researchers to be cognizant of, say, gendered assumptions.

## Participant-Observation

Genealogy tells us that scholars cannot avoid a role in linking power and morality, but analyses at the level of the international system tell little about the micro-level processes of socialization that reinforce institutionalized practices, traditional modes of thinking, and standard procedures for organizing knowledge. While constructivists insist that these practices can change, more often institutions provide stability to meanings by establishing norms that guide expectations and behavior. Most analyses, therefore, focus on those institutions, rather than the people who populate them. Before we can address the question of challenges to such rules, we must show how institutions are reproduced—how specific norms permeate institutional settings. Participant-observation allows researchers to see these processes more clearly, both in their own lives and in the international system.

At first glance participant-observation appears most congenial to studies of agency, but it can also be useful for understanding people within social or cultural contexts (Lichterman 2002). Because institutions socialize individual participants, bureaucracies replicate norms, and discourses reproduce power disparities through the active use of language, participant-observation pinpoints how practices are "instantiated" or embodied. Unfortunately, IR specialists rarely use it consciously as a method, even though service in government agencies has shaped many academics' beliefs about what is possible in world politics.

The writings of Cohn (1987) and Barnett (1993, 2002) detail the experiences that turned both scholars into cogs in the wheels that reproduce institutional practices. Cohn's work with nuclear weapons scientists and Barnett's time as a political officer for the United States at the United Nations reveal how specialized language socializes individuals into a bureaucracy. Cohn suggests four stages in the participant-observation process that also apply to Barnett's analysis: listening, speaking, dialogue, and "terror," a term she uses to indicate an unnerving alienation from former beliefs as the participant recognizes the internalization of the organization's alternate assumptions. These impacts of structure can by divided into two types: regulative ones that affect actions, and constitutive ones that affect identities.

### Regulative Effects

The initial period of listening to a new language and absorbing its rules was difficult for each new participant. When Cohn and Barnett arrived at their respective workplaces, they realized that their academic training and research experience did not prepare them for the new languages being spoken around them or the techniques for putting language into practice. Barnett lacked the knack for writing cables; he initially offered complex political science analyses rather than politically useful assessments of meetings. For Cohn, the sexual imagery inherent in the "technostrategic" language used by weapons scientists made her feel like an outsider. As a woman, using such sexually charged language had different implications for her than it did for her male colleagues.

Despite their handicaps, both learned to speak new languages and abide by new rules. They exhibited both professional and psychological motivations for doing so. Cohn, for example, points out that the scientists around her constantly used incomprehensible acronyms. If she hoped to understand them, she needed to learn their meanings. Furthermore, she found that when she purposely spoke "in English" after becoming proficient in techno-speak, even her most sophisticated questions got dismissed—unlike when she abided by the rules of the techno-language. Thus professional competency required learning institutional dialects. In addition, colleagues at both the weapons laboratory and the UN teased and cajoled both Cohn and Barnett about being outsiders. Personal acceptance required demonstrating an ability to fit into the local culture.

Both participant-observers draw out the moral implications of employing one discourse rather than another. Rather than questioning the validity of their own interpretations, both began from the ethical position that people must try to save human lives. Yet each found that employing the prevailing professional discourse provides all sorts of justifications for distancing oneself from the actual human lives in question. The UN discourse (as well as that of the US Mission to the UN) legitimized saving the reputation of the international organization over saving Rwandan lives. The weapons scientists' techno-speak discourse of a "second-strike capability" to counter an attack, even after the decimation of the country's population, legitimized military strategies that safeguard enough weapons to exact revenge. Clearly not everyone shared Cohn's and Barnett's perspectives on morality in these settings.

Cohn is interested in the "unreality" of the world constructed by techno-speak language. This language, populated by imagery and phraseology of dominance, paternalism, and sexuality, ironically also rationalizes and distances the user from any impact of these weapons on human lives. Thus nuclear strategists happily discuss war-fighting strategies and weapons' survivability without any attention to how the world populated by people might look if their war games were actually put into practice. The world constructed by the users of techno-speak is "real," but it bears little relationship to the world of a nuclear holocaust. The scientists and strategists have successfully isolated themselves from that latter world through the construction and use of a particular discourse. But we cannot dismiss this discourse as impracticable because it wields real power: it affects decision-making on resource-allocation and on the construction of actual bombs. Cohn's work demonstrates how discourses create new realities—moving analysts beyond regulative effects toward constitutive effects.

### Constitutive Effects

Most striking in these participant-observation accounts are descriptions of how the analysts' own thinking changed as a result of using specialized languages. Both Cohn and Barnett take seriously the transformative effects at the social-psychological level of learning the codes of an institutional discourse. They find the process of using a specialized language—engaging in dialogue—to be transformative, rather than simply a learning experience. Previously sympathetic to disarmament activists, Cohn discovered that she got so caught up in the justifications for new weapons systems that she almost forgot how to articulate her long-standing critiques of strategic thinking. (Gusterson [1996] describes a similar shift after a long period of interviewing nuclear weapons scientists.) Barnett, in turn, found himself articulating a version of US national interests that meshed best with the values of the "international community," as represented by the UN. Over time, these participant-observers found themselves making unfamiliar arguments and asking profoundly different questions than they had before learning their bureaucratic dialects. In less than a year, both Cohn and Barnett had been socialized into their respective languages and argumentation processes.

In the end, perhaps because of their relatively short stints working in these institutions, both remained critical of the position promoted by their respective bureaucracies. Both also say that this very process of stepping back—trying to resist the force of socialization at the end of their year-long assignments—proved quite difficult and only partially successful. Cohn describes experiencing "terror" when she assessed her participant-observer experience. Similarly, Barnett, having participated in the UN decision not to send a peacekeeping force to Rwanda at the height of the 1994 genocide, now decries the sense of indifference that his institutional role taught him. He went on to research the "pathologies" of international organizations (Barnett and Finnemore 1999, 2004). Cohn pondered whether peace activists ought to learn techno-speak in order to be taken more seriously by scientists and policymakers or, alternatively, to highlight irrationalities like the sexual imagery she discovered, in order to undermine the legitimacy of the language itself and the strategic analysts who speak it.

Barnett is less focused on the creation of a separate techno-strategic world through language and more interested in how institutional discourses create perceptions of "interests" that become consistently reproduced in institutional decision-making. In the case of the UN, the perceived interest in the organization's reputation (and not incurring another peacekeeping "loss") trumped the worry about mass killings of Rwandans. Rather than language being part of the creation of a new world, here language constructs interests that isolate an organization from the chaos of an already existing world. A few particular words such as genocide become critically important (and disallowed) because they have the power to disrupt the isolation constructed by bureaucratic discourse.

Language is thus intimately tied to ethics. Only by appealing to the "higher" moral authority based on the values of the international community did UN decision-makers legitimize their failure to act in Rwanda. Nuclear strategists can cope with the horrors of nuclear war scenarios only by domesticating weapons, removing people from the equations, and making the weapons' security the most legitimate goal. These studies of the disciplining power of language within bureaucracies complement traditional reliance on interviews and archives. Together with the longer historical perspectives offered by genealogy and macro-historical comparisons, this approach demonstrates some of the relationships between social and material structures, as well as the problem-solving implications of a critical response to institutionalized theoretical assumptions (cf. Cox 1986).

## Implications

A constructivist ontology of mutual constitution challenges structuralism (of various kinds) by bringing back a role for agency in the *reproduction* of social orders. No ideology automatically becomes an integral part of an actor's understanding of the world; people's words and behavior reinforce particular meanings, which often become taken-for-granted assumptions. As process-oriented methodologies, macro-historical comparison, genealogy, and participant-observation illustrate how actors frequently reinforce the institutionalized meanings and practices that comprise structures. Certainly these are not the only methods available to examine systems, regimes, and bureaucracies, nor are these methods confined to the analysis of these institutional forms or effects. We selected these three approaches because they highlight structural malleability rather than stasis and, therefore, offer a way to tease out constitutive processes at the heart of the agent-structure debate.

Most of the studies that we surveyed here take for granted the European roots of the contemporary international system. Not surprisingly, many of these scholars have drawn upon and critiqued the "English School" approach, which has been criticized for basing its conceptualization of international society solely on European history. Further work on structure would benefit from branching out to cover more thoroughly different types of social orders defined in their own terms (e.g., Ling 2002). This is not to say that constructivists should abandon the study of Europe and the United States, but simply that we should continue to question the field's tendency to define European orders as the norm. While avoiding the reification of civilizations, we might include more in-depth accounts of Asia, Africa, or the Americas that go beyond religious conflicts at the heart of the Crusades or practices of colonial exploration. Such analyses might also explore the implications of alternative "moral orders," including gendered social structures, across macro-historical periods and within specific organizations (e.g., Goldstein 2001).

Particularly in the current phase of globalization, it is problematic to study any type of system in isolation. Anthropologists, for example, have more or less forsaken the search for "untouched" cultures. Instead, they increasingly conduct ethnographic research to explore the connections between local and global practices (Gupta and Ferguson, eds. 1997). Given IR's focus on political authority in the form of global governance and the state as intermediary between processes that link global and local practices, constructivists are well positioned to contribute insights about the extent to which globalization may be reducing the possibility of alternative social orders. Barnett's participant-observation at the UN offers but one example of how an ethnographic perspective can demonstrate the tensions between universal and local languages. Even techno-speak is a version of English. To grapple with research spanning social, spatial, and historical settings, constructivists must speak multiple languages to employ any type of discursive method.

Thus far, we have tried to isolate, as much as possible, the institutional side of the agent-structure relationship. Inevitably, we have underplayed agency in this chapter, even though we have shied away from deterministic arguments and encouraged greater use of participant-observation. But language is both a source of continuity within institutions and a mechanism for individual change. Not every action reinforces prevailing ideologies; actors can also transform prevailing practices. We turn, therefore, to concepts and tools better suited to capturing agency.

# Chapter Three

# **Agency**

At first glance, the very mention of agency appears to set up an opposition to structure. Presumably structure is static, while agency moves. But this dichotomy does not fully capture the constructivist perspective. Discourses establish an actor's place in the world. As the participant-observation studies of Chapter 2 demonstrated, informal rules and formal bureaucracies create frameworks of meaning within which people think and act. Their actions, in turn, can support or oppose these dominant discourses. Perhaps someone offers a new discourse at a time of crisis, making it more persuasive than the prevailing one. These new rules and procedures may shift people's worldviews. When people speak and write to convey these new meanings, they again replicate identities and practices through their language, creating a cycle of mutual constitution. As a result, actors and institutions are not discrete entities, because they are constituted by each other.

This inherent inseparability of language, practices, identities, and institutions presents challenges for researching the relationship between structure and agency. Constitutive processes, such as socialization, affect national leaders, governments, social movements, classes, gendered people, corporations, and intergovernmental organizations at different times and in different ways. Historical comparisons may focus scholarly attention on the emergence of new practices at particular moments, but even genealogy, which highlights exceptional disjunctures, underplays agency in favor of documenting shifts in discourse. Researchers need methodologies that better capture people's decisions and motivations to provide an alternative to a rational-choice model based on utility-maximization by pre-formed individuals in the context of structural constraints. Constructivists do not need one overarching theory of agency, but we do need a better understanding of the underlying assumptions that lead to diverse conceptualizations of it, for these require choices between alternative methodologies.

Constructivists start from the assumption that human beings, including researchers, have purposes and goals, or "intentions." They act on behalf of themselves as individuals and as members of (formal and informal) groups. By arguing and demanding, they advance their views of the world. These intentions and interpretations affect whether (and when) people choose to stimulate, prod, foster, block, revolutionize, produce, reproduce, legitimize, delegitimize, destroy, or rebuild structures. Methodologies that highlight reasoning and communication best capture these processes of construction, deconstruction, and reconstruction. We start with historical narrative, which draws attention to the ways in which scholars privilege certain actors and contextualize them to make sense of their stories. To capture more of these actors' choices and strategies, we turn to framing, an approach common in sociology, which differentiates between legitimate and illegitimate types of political claims. Finally, we draw lessons from ethnography, the traditional method of anthropologists, to concentrate on the relationship between individuals and communities. Acknowledging the ability of both actors on the world stage and those who analyze them to transcend or overturn dominant discourses also raises issues of accountability and ethics.

## Narrative

Narratives highlight the agency of particular individuals or groups by telling a story with a plot and main characters (White 1987; Patterson and Monroe 1998). Its classic use in IR is diplomatic history, where scholars construct stories about state leaders, such as Alexander the Great, Napoleon, Bismarck, Wilson, Hitler, Churchill, Nasser, Gandhi, Kennedy, and Mandela. But narrative can be much more than a "great man" view of history. Others use it to highlight the attempts of social movements to shape international regimes governing the environment, peace, security, and human rights. In telling (rival) stories, researchers might employ metaphors to convey heroism or tragedy, verbs that celebrate the role of non-governmental organizations in setting agendas, or the passive voice to reflect policy effects.

By writing a particular plot, the analyst creates an argument about influences or outcomes. Unlike genealogy, which stresses disjunctures, plots develop a storyline, with a beginning and, arguably, an end (Halttunen 1999). Scholars disagree about whether these plots create causal claims (Barnett 1998; Lynch 1999a; Suganami 1999), echoing the positivist and post-positivist positions that we identified in Chapter 1. Some make a case for complex and context-sensitive multi-causal analysis, while others insist that the recursive nature of constitutive processes precludes distinctions between discrete variables. (We return to the suggestion that these be treated as "feedback loops" in Chapter 4.) Thus some narratives offer a dramatic retelling of history, while others present an explicit causal analysis. Either way, the analyst emphasizes key actors in an unfolding drama.

### The Cast of Characters

Analytical categories, such as state, class, gender, or leader, create actors and relationships between them. Non-state actors, for instance, may be called non-governmental organizations, networks, social movements, epistemic communities, moral entrepreneurs, or even "civil society." Each of these designations emphasizes different dimensions to the group. Advocacy networks form around principled ideas or values that inspire their actions and shape their organizations (Keck and Sikkink 1998), in contrast to interest groups which presumably unite on the basis of instrumental goals. (In practice it is often difficult to apply this differentiation.) Interest groups and social movements, in turn, serve as nodes in advocacy networks. Focusing on movements rather than networks highlights the difference between those working through state bureaucracies and those seeking change from outside formal political institutions. Moral entrepreneurs can range from charismatic individuals to social movements to innovative corporations.

The lack of clear boundaries between these groups and organizations reinforces the need to think of them as socially constructed through narratives—both the ones they adopt and those applied to them by commentators. The contested term "civil society" illustrates this point. Some activists and scholars attribute agency to "global civil society," citing its capacity for significant influence. In this usage, global civil society consists of non-governmental organizations (NGOs), social movements, and mass publics interacting with elites in ways that collectively push forward debate and decision-making on issues such as peace, the environment, and human rights (Kaldor 2003; Wapner 1996; Schmitz 2006). This view emphasizes the synergies (or rivalries) between groups and attributes intentionality to them. (Some also debate the use of the adjective "global" to characterize civil society; see, for example, Haynes 1997 and Wiarda 2003.)

Other scholars employ the term to connote a social space, or "public sphere," in which groups such as NGOs, networks, and social movements act, calling attention to the context that shapes the interactions between them (Cohen and Arato 1992; Keane 1998). This choice of terminology shifts our focus to the discursive construction of subjectivity. Subjectivity refers to the role of social practices, rather than psychological processes, in constituting individuals and groups. Discourses shape people's mindsets, worldviews, and goals in more-or-less unconscious ways, leading them to act through habit and influencing their more conscious choices. Intentional action, in contrast, implies a more explicit wish to influence the understandings and behavior of others. The degree to which people can act intentionally despite their construction as subjects is a matter of debate. In other words, the notion of subjectivity holds implications for how much causal weight analysts attribute to actors and the ethical judgments they make about actions (issues we return to below).

Because core categorizations can also marginalize certain actors, alternative concepts and methods can highlight other actors.

In state-centric diplomatic history, for example, narratives focus primarily on men as leaders, and generally treat the actions prized by these leaders (showing "resolve," making "credible threats," and refusing to be seen as "weak") as necessary and normal. In contrast, gender scholars employ alternative narratives to demonstrate the often-unseen roles of women, as well as the alternative types of actions and values (cooperation, mutual assistance) that both women and men can practice. Gender scholars also point to the common distinction between public and private spheres of action that privilege men as the actors who matter in international security and the global economy (Tickner 1992, 2001; Sylvester 1994; Peterson and Runyan, 1999; Robinson, 1999; Peterson 2003). To provide a more complete story of the gendered nature of the global economy or international negotiations, one which includes actions within the private sphere, scholars have written about (among others) home-workers (Prügl 1999) and wives of diplomats (Enloe 1993).

## *Storylines*

Theoretical frameworks guide the selection of adjectives to describe actors and verbs to indicate the nature of their agency. Active verbs, for instance, convey agency, whereas the passive voice may imply the salience of structural conditions. Scholars usually compare their resulting storylines with other existing or hypothetical ones, at times leading to the identification of logical gaps. Narrative illustrates how constructivists use logical inference to judge analysis.

After proclaiming a particular narrative problematic, the researcher must figure out whether and how to tell a better story. Following traditional standards of historiography, a good story is coherent and incorporates a wide variety of types of evidence. Those who reject narratives of statesmen as too gendered, for instance, require extensive documentation of the characteristics and activities of a plethora of individuals, informal groups, nongovernmental organizations and inter-governmental bureaucracies to construct alternative narratives. One of the most common strategies is to use societal voices as a check on the views of elites in

government or business. These analyses help analysts understand
the means by which some actors attempt to transcend (gendered)
forms of power or create autonomous spaces for action (a point
we return to below).

Since government sources generally favor state-centric and
elite analyses, demonstrating that non-state actors somehow matter requires alternative sources of information. Documentation
can be limited for innumerable reasons, not least the absence of
government funding for archives about the activities of people
who remain hidden from official view. For instance, the historical
contributions of interwar peace movements to international organizations are often buried in official documents. Brushing off the
archival dust of the Cold War reveals their role (Lynch 1999a). In
the new millennium, it has become easier to learn about non-state
actors in the official materials covering, say, United Nations conferences on the environment (Rio), housing (Istanbul), women's
rights (Beijing), human rights (Vienna), and the idea of a "social
contract" (Copenhagen). Informal sources often supplement these
official documents. Whenever possible, researchers should conduct interviews with participants and pour over media coverage,
newsletters, editorials, and minutes of meetings. The internet now
offers quick and cheap access to a wide range of potential source
materials, including tracts of activists who target multinational
corporations and international financial institutions, as well as
responses from the World Bank, the International Monetary Fund,
and the International Labor Organization.

Additional resources do not eliminate all the difficulties inherent
in uncovering the "hidden transcripts" (Scott 1990) of the views
of silenced actors. While the advent of the internet solves some
of these issues, not all activists, such as illiterate peasants in rural
areas, possess the resources—or have the inclination—to post
electronically. Women in the private sphere may leave no records
of their work planning the informal gatherings that facilitate formal
agreements. Radical voices that challenge the status quo, such as
home-workers protesting labor conditions, get even less credit for
any influence on policy. Interviews may be impossible, especially
for historical movements and when potential interlocutors live in

fear. Telling a more complete story, therefore, depends in part on employing creative techniques to gather a broad array of evidence (Reinharz 1992; Clemens and Hughes 2002).

Conversely, relying only on societal views can lead to an over-estimation of the effectiveness of social movements. Since elites and social movements naturally discount the significance of each other to bolster their own importance, analysts should balance self-perceptions against assessments by representatives of other government agencies, officials in international organizations, public opinion polls, and people working in affiliated or competing non-governmental organizations. Diverse viewpoints should be compared to weigh the evidence, to enhance the coherence of a new story, and to see which theory leads to a more logical or inclusive plot. Since narratives are interpretations, rather than "correct" stories based on objective facts, their coherence and completeness are often challenged.

## *Meta-Narratives*

Since analysts write narratives by drawing on theories that reflect dominant ideologies, researchers themselves become characters in "meta-narratives." Some forms of (generally post-positivist) scholarship critique meta-narratives directly, analyzing the relationships that enable their construction and reproduction. Striving to expose hidden biases, other writers purposely use stories about marginalized actors, such as women or peace movements, as a tool of empowerment. Not surprisingly, these reinterpretations tend to go against the grain of traditional scholarship. Still other researchers may remain unconsciously embedded in ideological assumptions. For example, Lynch (1999a) points out that previous studies persisted in explaining the onset of World War II by blaming interwar peace movements for policies of appeasement and isolationism, even though these same studies primarily stressed structural economic or strategic factors that preclude a significant explanatory role for non-state actors. She links these inconsistencies to the perpetuation of a Realist worldview among both politicians and analysts that conceives of social movements in negative terms.

Thus discursive power takes two forms within the narrative method, one that uses concepts to construct and contextualize agency through storylines and another which draws on broader ideologies to privilege certain plots over others. Meta-narratives provide insight into the broader impact of theoretical assumptions. For example, one might view the contemporary attention to non-state actors as reflecting the dominance of Western liberalism in the aftermath of the collapse of communism as an alternative worldview. Moreover, liberalism's emphasis on democratic governance and market economies, according to this argument, privileges certain identities and definitions of threat, which in turn affect who gets foreign aid and in what form. For others, the concern is less whether liberalism represents Western domination and more how its practices open up or close spaces for non-state actors to influence policy in the direction of "progress." Any definition of progress is, of course, value-laden.

Liberalism, or any other form of discursive dominance, shuts down alternative ways of thinking and acting. Reproduction of institutionalized practices leaves little room for change, including within the academy, because silent assumptions naturalize conventional perspectives. This necessitates a better understanding of how academics reproduce or transcend particular ideological positions. Therefore, narrative as an analytical tool becomes a form of political action. By highlighting these two levels of interpretation, this method draws attention to the question of what actors—including academics—seek to achieve. The method of framing helps researchers identify the purposes and effects of such action.

## Framing

As analysts trying to understand why people do what they do, and whether they succeed in what they hope to achieve, constructivists explore the use of discourses and the diverse effects of actions. A traditional policy-oriented view tends to evaluate effectiveness (or influence, or power) based on an actor's ability to achieve goals through instrumental action. Attention to the way actors construct meanings broadens our understanding of both goals and means to include attempts to alter the language used in policy debates. Since meanings are the basis for actions, it becomes difficult to distinguish instrumental and constitutive dynamics. For example, a discursive goal might be to change people's awareness about an issue through the instrumental manipulation of religious, ethnic, or historical symbols (Brysk 1993, 2000), thus challenging assumptions about what it means for actors to be "rational" or "self-interested."

Frame analysis, which developed primarily as a reaction against materialist and rationalist assumptions in the social movement field (Goffman 1974; Snow and Benford 1988), attempts to disentangle this complex relationship between actors, goals, and behavior by concentrating on the production of meaning as a type of influence. Its application to, say, transnational social movements seeking to influence international organizations and states within international regimes, involves two steps. Researchers first delve into the production of discourse through content analysis of specific frames. Then they evaluate the impacts of these frames on actions. Accommodating both the discursive and behavioral dimensions of those impacts requires expanded measures of success and failure.

## Content Analysis

A more specific form of discourse than ideology, a frame describes concrete situations in ways that legitimate specific objectives and actions. The boundaries between types of discourse blurs with the profusion of labels such as "master frame" or "meta-cultural frame" serving much the same purpose as "ideology" or "discourse." Others prefer to use "narrative" for the claims of actors as well as for historical analyses (Bosia 2005). Indeed, the images that leaders and activists invoke are components of both frames and broader ideologies. To minimize confusion and to highlight disciplinary differences, in this discussion we use the sociological term "frame" specifically to denote a template that identifies a problem and offers a solution (within the context of broader theoretical and ideological assumptions). A substantial amount of research on the activities of "epistemic communities," for instance, has traced discourses of knowledge and their impact on policies in the areas of the environment, human rights, security, and economic governance—a broad scope of issues covered by international regimes.

Although the concept took hold in social movement theory, its applicability is not limited to any particular type of actor. Both activists and policy-makers articulate their analysis of a problem and ways to resolve it by seeking to generate agreement and support, often strategizing extensively over the selection of a frame (Schön and Rein 1994). Presenting a frame in a way that resonates with a broader audience may necessitate a strategic assessment of the role of the media, since most actors strive to obtain coverage to publicize their positions and to compete with rival frames. Potential audiences include mass publics, experts, and policy-makers at sub-national, national, transnational, and global levels.

To identify these frames, researchers start with much of the same evidence used in other discursive methods, such as statements of leaders, minutes of group meetings, publicity materials, and press treatments of the message. The main difference is the explicit focus on action in distilling these materials. The analyst seeks to identify a basic template that designates an actor's view of a fairly narrow issue, particular grievances, potential opponents, and other key assumptions that reflect strategies for maneuvering through the policy-making process and promoting specific prescriptions for action. For example, many US peace activists, along with some international lawyers and scientists, articulated a "common security" frame during the Cold War, which argued in favor of international control of nuclear weapons and against the view that US security was separable from that of the rest of the world (Meyer 1990; Gamson 1992; Knopf 1998). Within the United States and Europe, scientists and elites who worked to slow the superpower arms race, as well as grassroots activists critical of the nuclear doctrine of Mutual Assured Destruction, consistently reiterated this common security frame.

Typologies and various qualitative or quantitative coding procedures reveal patterns in the evidence. To start, researchers look for particular words or terms that express normative goals linked to policy prescriptions. For example, in newsletters, pamphlets, signs, and webpages, social movements might pair "globalization" (and

similar terms) with other key words that assign a positive or negative value to it. Depending on the volume of information, a selective
sampling may be necessary. Some texts, such as UN documents,
rely on formulaic presentations, which make it easier to identify
patterns. Increasingly sophisticated computer programs also enable
better context-sensitive coding of large amounts of information,
which can provide useful supplements to qualitative analyses.
Analysts might also include non-written forms of discourse, such
as the clothing worn by protestors, as alternative "texts." These
would require the application of other visually oriented techniques
to interpret meanings.

Content analysis can then be put into historical perspective to
track how specific terms take on a particular salience at given points
in time and whether their use spreads geographically. Contrasting
frames by situating one against its alternatives adds depth to the
analysis and precludes the risk of arbitrarily designating a single
frame "strong" or "weak." Comparing how widely used one or
another frame may be is one metric for assessing which is more (or
less) dominant. Contrasting these frames also shows interactions
between them. Frames do not necessarily develop in isolation; rivalries may even produce "frame wars" (Di Alto 2004). One frame
can illuminate some of the discursive techniques (including the
demonstration of logical inconsistencies) that groups can employ
to distinguish or subordinate an alternative frame. For example,
Eastern Europe and Soviet dissidents in the 1980s struggled to link
peace with human rights, while their governments strove to keep
peace exclusively a problem of nuclear weapons and anti-missile
defense systems. Not surprisingly, this broader perspective reveals
that frames do not always come in neat and coherent packages,
nor do actors necessarily promote only one frame. Frames can be
overlapping and layered, with varying degrees of consistency or
coherence. Explicitly mapping these layers and the connections
between specific frames is one strategy for coping with this complexity (Johnston 2002).

Because it primarily relies on actors' own representations of
a situation, frame analysis highlights instrumental agency more
than narrative, which constructs situated or contextualized stories

about people's actions. But the frame analyst remains embedded in meta-narratives or master-frames that are often left unquestioned; the broader ideological context in which scholars work draws our attention to some frames more readily than others. Some researchers may be more inductive than others in identifying frames, but any type of analysis that assigns meanings relies, at least to some extent, on theoretically derived categories to put words or clothing into social and historical context. The frame analyst, like the writer of narratives, may also be drawn to particular interpretations for normative reasons. Meta-narrative analysis reminds us that nothing inherently privileges one frame or actor over another.

### *Assessing Effects*

Perhaps the most basic level at which analysts should attribute success to an actor is when its frame becomes predominant. At a minimum, researchers can document the extent to which the key words of one frame appear in the discourse of other actors, and trace the timing of the appearance of these words in policy debates to confirm that the discourse indeed originated with the first actor (Rochon 1998). For example, human rights and peace groups helped tear down the Berlin Wall, both literally and figuratively, by expressing the societal dissatisfaction that delegitimized communist regimes and contributed to the end of the bipolar system (Thomas 2001; Beissinger 2002). It is important to keep in mind that logical consistency within a frame need not be a prerequisite for its strength or dominance. However, inconsistencies may create vulnerabilities which detractors can target to undermine it.

Recognizing contestation brings the researcher back to the relationship between the frame and its proponents. Analysts need to be clear whether (or when) to attribute "success" to the ideas within a frame or to the people who promote them. While a frame may develop something of a life of its own, like norms and rules that get institutionalized, actors still need to articulate these discourses, either to confirm or challenge them. Proponents can be societal actors or governing elites, or some combination. For example, environmental epistemic communities produce specialized forms of knowledge about global warming that can be transmitted to elites and bureaucrats, as well as social movements. Some of these groups may work through established political channels, while others opt for demonstrations, marches, and open meetings to get their messages across to broader publics. Researchers can then examine the degree of correspondence between the content of a particular frame and any of its proponents. Analysts should not presume that social movements and elites necessarily work in opposition to each other; this is an empirical question. With so many potential proponents of the same frame (or close variants of it), one needs to be cautious about attributing "success" to only a few actors in creating an influential frame.

Constructivists should remain sensitive to the goal-specific nature of any evaluation. Because actors use frames "to mobilize potential adherents and constituents, to garner bystander support, and to demobilize antagonists" (Snow and Benford 1988: 198), success for a social movement might be affirmation of its foundational grievances, even in the absence of any adoption of its policy prescriptions, because the frame creates a persuasive articulation of a problem. In contrast, a somewhat dysfunctional outcome would be a movement that attracts new members only by significantly shifting away from its basic values. Other actors, such as political parties or interest groups, may be inherently more instrumental than principled in setting their goals, in which case gains like strategic membership increases might not be judged as a failure even if accompanied by a shift in values.

In addition, analysts should remember that not all actors seek change, and their frames can (successfully) reinforce the status quo. Ruling elites, for instance, might use frames to deflect demands from social movements. And bureaucrats may not even be aware that they are using frames that have become embedded in policy discourses. Frequently people tacitly reproduce established ways of doing things. For example, US citizens who do not exercise their right to vote tacitly support their government's policies and, by extension, contribute to the reproduction of dominant power relations in the world. In addition, understanding that the state in Eastern Europe provided healthcare, education, and jobs helps to explain how post Cold War voters, in a market-oriented environment, could return communists or socialists to power.

We have focused our discussion on intentions, but actions can also have unintended consequences of various kinds. For example, crackdowns on political expression can, paradoxically, encourage people to create covert spaces for cultural and political dialogue that strengthen civil societies against repressive states. Promoting individual and political rights can broaden voting participation while leaving intact extreme economic inequalities. The search by businesses for ever-cheaper labor in poor countries may encourage transnational forms of union organizing. As always, analysts should be careful when inferring motivations from such unexpected outcomes. However, asking whether actors should be held accountable for such unintended effects raises questions about taking "intentionality" as the starting point for conceptualizing agency. We turn to ethnography as one tool to probe this issue.

**Ethnography**

Constructivists are certainly not the first to grapple with the relationship between individuals and society. Marxists ponder class consciousness and highlight the role of multinational corporations as manifestations of a collective bourgeois interest. Liberals explore the formation and impacts of interest groups. Sociologists probe collective identity as a basis for (ethnic, racial, religious, gendered) mobilization and networking. Rational choice analysts and cognitive psychologists, in different ways, start with individuals as the unit of analysis in social interactions. Rather than simply adding more actors to this analytical mix, constructivism conceives of agency as interacting with meanings. Structures both constitute actors and limit the range of their actions.

Ethnography, a combination of participant-observation and interviewing, is a method useful for developing a contemporaneous, people-centered understanding of societies at the local level, particularly as it takes seriously everyday voices and practices within a broader discursive context. Ethnographers traditionally engage in intensive on-site observation and inquiry to ascertain what practices "mean," what rules and norms people follow, and what institutions result. In this vein, the work of anthropologist Clifford Geertz (e.g., 1973, 1983) has had an extraordinarily wide impact across the social sciences and humanities. Until recently (e.g., Hopf 2002), IR has remained less affected, perhaps because the ethnographer's archetypal research site was an "indigenous" village presumably far removed from the influences of the international system. As the field increasingly accepts the importance of elite as well as non-elite actors, the boundaries of legitimate study have expanded to include bureaucracies and international organizations. Ethnography is an appropriate tool for probing the nature of agency in these settings. This requires an appreciation of people as subjects rather than objects of research. Dialogues with these interlocutors, furthermore, can lead to transformations in consciousness.

## *Subjectivity*

Jepperson, Wendt, and Katzenstein (1996: 41) address the issue of the relationship between individuals and their communities by differentiating three ways in which "environments" affect actors, which they see as "progressively higher levels of 'construction.'" At the highest level, environments affect the existence of actors. Going back to our examples of diplomatic wives and home-workers, gender permits people with certain biological features (labeled men) to be actors in world affairs, but not those (women) who lack those physical characteristics. In a genderless world, one would not see a pattern of biological difference in who occupies these roles. The middle level concerns the properties of actors, such as their identities, interests, and capabilities. A deeply gendered environment would lead women to become wives rather than diplomats and home-workers rather than corporate executives, due to differential access to education and myriad many other discriminatory factors. Finally, environments have behavioral implications. If women are encouraged to avoid conflict, for instance, home-workers are unlikely to go on strike and wives of ambassadors are unlikely to demand their own careers as diplomats.

Many constructivists concentrate on the middle and lowest levels of construction, studying the properties and behavior of actors, such as the formation of interests and the impact of norms. Others, however, probe the deeper questions of "existence" that precede these more-specific research agendas. For example, postcolonial studies build on Said's (1978) critique of the way that colonizers and Western academics embedded descriptions of Arabs as inferior "Orientals" in their writings and policy recommendations. Western notions of sovereignty have subsequently shaped the self-understandings of post-colonial nationalist Arab leaders such as Gamal Abdel Nasser in Egypt and Saddam Hussein in Iraq. These leaders' self-understandings reflect the modernist secular discourse of sovereignty, even though Islamist movements have resisted it (Eickelman 1997; Salvatore and LeVine, eds. 2005).

Challenging anthropology's traditional penchant for objectifying an exotic "other," followers of Foucault in particular concentrate on three practices that produce the "constitution of the subject" (Dreyfus and Rabinow 1982; Latour 1993). Elites and societies practice categorization and classification. The physical division of some groups of people from others allows for isolation or confinement of those whom society treats as objects, such as the poor, the ill, and the insane. Scientific classification reinforces hierarchies between these categories, such as "workers" above "prisoners," or "men" over "women." Finally, "subjectification" requires people to engage in "self-formation" by their reiteration of the discourses of social hierarchy. Because the notion of subjectivity connects an actor's intentions and practices, it becomes a focal point for analyzing and critiquing the mechanisms, or "techniques," of power that link individuals and societies.

Others find the notion of subjectivity problematic, since it tends to treat actors as almost entirely shaped by dominant discourses, downplaying their own role in replicating those practices (Milliken 1999). Constructivism's ontological assumption that structure and agency are mutually constituted implies that people are both socialized into their situations and capable of transformative actions. This view grants more significance to agency than found in some of the more structuralist readings of Foucault that focus on how techniques of discursive power define subjects (see Suggested Readings). This tension can be acknowledged (if not resolved) in empirical research by exploring the degree to which actors are capable of transcending their subject positions. Agents do not "possess" individual intentionality as a characteristic or inherent property—individualism is a construction of the modernist era (Taylor 2001).

By defining agency in terms of intentionality, constructivists presume that people are at least partially capable of perceiving and assessing the structures within which they act. The question remains whether a researcher can ever truly understand another person's perspective. Even "experience-near" concepts do not enable analysts to perceive the world in the same ways that research subjects do (Geertz 1979). Constructivism needs to delve further into the notion of consciousness in order to grasp how people conceive of themselves within historically specific contexts of social hierarchy.

## Consciousness

Ethnographic methods are premised upon a relationship between the observer and the observed. Participant-observation, introduced in Chapter 2, is one of its tools, semi-structured interviews the other. (For basic guidelines on non-elite interviewing, as well as some of the limitations of structured interviews, see Blee and Taylor 2002.) These need not be treated as two separate techniques, since more extensive interaction through participant-observation may build trust that enhances the interviews (indeed, unstructured interviews blur the distinction). Both techniques are also premised on the researcher's immersion in secondary histories and, when appropriate, language proficiency. The biggest challenge is to *listen*, since researchers inevitably bring their own theoretical and cultural assumptions to this encounter.

To illustrate, we draw on feminist scholarship, which has long questioned the objectification of women. Analysis of gendered power relations is an inherently ethical task that seeks lessons for emancipatory action (Fraser 1989). Both scholars and activists of transnational women's rights, for example, criticize the ways that

Western discourses frame problems and solutions for women. In response, Ackerly (2000) and Sandoval (2000) combine descriptive, analytical, and normative elements to highlight the voices of "Third World" women, who advocate goals such as participation, social justice, democracy, and basic needs. Their analyses link an ethic of social justice to the agency of marginalized women, demonstrating ways that intentional action can transcend the limitations enshrined in dominant subjectivities. This skeptical "scrutiny" (Ackerly's term) of emancipatory discourses for marginalized women is part of a process of social transformation that "decolonizes the imagination" (Sandoval's phrase).

Yet any social change risks instituting new forms of dominance and inequality. This is also a central problem of cosmopolitanism in political theory (e.g., Ishay 1995; Lynch 1999b). Talk of women's rights can essentialize some gendered characteristics at the expense of others. Not all women support the rights codified in the UN Convention on the Elimination of All Forms of Discrimination against Women, for instance. The challenge is to encourage steps toward something which might be called social justice, while allowing women in specific situations (such as South Asia and the United States, respectively, in Ackerly's and Sandoval's books) to define its meaning for themselves. To this end, both Ackerly and Sandoval self-consciously choose the label "Third World" as a reflection of these women's own articulations of their subjectivities. Both also discuss the controversies surrounding the label "feminist" in these activist communities. This is one small step toward allowing women to analyze their own situations and to transcend obstacles to their own empowerment. It moves analysis away from subjectivity defined by meanings and values imposed from outside (be it the "developed world," the "North," or the "West") and creates openings for ethical judgment by actors as well as scholars.

As an outside observer, Ackerly favors consulting local activists to develop criteria for challenging existing practices and norms; a process she calls engaging in "deliberative inquiry" with "social critics." She argues that analysts must continually tack back and forth between universal lists and local priorities. Disagreements arise, for instance, over the value of self-employment versus unionized work.

Her own criteria derive from interpretations and priorities set by lo-cal activists, who enact, embody, and revise their own articulations of their rights and objectives. Thus she compares the priorities set in UN conferences gleaned from covenants and treaties to what she learns through interviews and position papers about the positions of the Self-Employed Women's Association in Gujarat, India and the network of Women Living Under Muslim Laws, two groups which did not participate in those international meetings. Sandoval also recommends greater attention to popular culture as a form of resistance, particularly in its expressions of parody and satire.

Feminist social criticism locates its potential for empowerment and ethical action in this process of democratic deliberation, which Sandoval calls the development of a coalitional consciousness. Ob-servers should engage in dialogue with those such as Sandoval, who have experiences as both insiders and outsiders (based on geography, ethnicity, education, class, profession, or other lines of distinction). For example, a black woman from Africa who has been educated in Western Europe and returns to run a local NGO can be such a "multi-sited critic," as would a Muslim-American anthropologist researching veiling practices in the Middle East. Moreover, research-ers need to go beyond the analysis of whether or not women achieve their goals (as in frame analysis) to view the process of delibera-tion as always a work-in-progress. This reflexivity, along with the incorporation of multi-sited social critics, aims to guard against the creation of new forms of unequal power relations.

Thus far constructivists have tended to focus on actors with whom analysts themselves sympathize. While this helps bridge the gap between an observer's understanding of the observed's percep-tions, it also potentially blinds the analyst to the possible negative implications of actions by supposedly "good" social movements and advocacy networks. Greater attention to bottom-up strategies gives voice to those silenced by discursive hierarchies, but feminists may propagate new empowerment norms that, ironically, continue to objectify poor women. These same methods can also be used to grapple with "bad" social causes, such as the ones that result in genocide or other forms of racism.

Ultimately, all evaluations of actors and their practices contain implicit and explicit normative positions, many of which will be arbitrated by the narratives scholars write that privilege some issues and actions over others. Nothing about the constructivist understanding of the constitutive relationship between agency and structure predicts the ethical position of the analysts or the subject of research (Adler 1997; Wilmer 2002). Researchers should remain attuned to the ethical implications of how they frame their questions and pursue answers.

## Implications

Our aim in this chapter has been to establish a role for agency in the context of structures and processes of mutual constitution. Actors constantly negotiate, reproduce, or change meanings. Insistence on people's intentionality also contains an inherent ethical component. But the constitutive effects of structure operate at different levels of analysis, leading analysts to disagree about the locus of agency and hence accountability. Models that replicate IR's traditional focus on the state as a single unit give them personality through concepts such as "state identity" (Wendt 1999). Some shift attention to the context in which states interact, by including international organizations and communities of experts, such as scientists and lawyers, as agents that communicate specialized forms of knowledge (Haas, ed. 1992; Finnemore 1996). Opening up the state to look at elite discourses leads quickly to the question of individuals as actors, the conventional locus of morality.

While studies of social movements and non-governmental organizations demonstrate the influence of people ignored in the state-centric approaches, there are no clear-cut or inherent boundaries between intra-state and inter-state elites or between members of national and transnational societies. Movements link activists across civil societies, while elite networks can include bureaucrats within states. Individuals frequently travel between government and the private sector, from movements and networks to official positions in international organizations. Therefore, constructivists should hold all people, not only elites, responsible for maintaining the world as it is, even if they replicate prevailing practices out of habit.

By critiquing histories of and by elites, constructivists challenge interpretations that marginalize or silence some actors. Narrative, framing, and ethnography expose this discursive power more explicitly than other methods, because they draw attention to the attribution of agency to people (both as individuals and in groups) through language and symbols that stress certain characters and downplay others. Stories and frames constructed by both participants and analysts convey these meanings in terms of action. But it is not enough to say that agency matters. We have paid little attention in this chapter to differences among actors and motivations for their actions. For instance, we have used gender as a category without probing its intersections with class, ethnicity, religion, race, or other classifications.

Therefore, in the next chapter, we turn to the properties of actors, examining how identities define individuals as members of collectivities and how these translate into actions. In the process, we draw out some of the abiding tensions between conceptions of agency based on subjectivity, where identities such as race and gender are primarily imposed by societal discourses, and those based on rationality, which stress that people select their identities, such as religion and ethnicity, as the product of instrumental calculations.

# Chapter Four

# Identities

In keeping with an ontology of mutual constitution of agents and structures, constructivists view identities as social relationships that change over time and across contexts. For instance, threats to security demarcate enemies, thus creating the categories of Self and Other that define identities. Because they are relationships, identities are not immutable characteristics of individuals or groups; people produce and reproduce them, rather than being born with them. In empirical research, therefore, constructivists explore the processes that link contexts and actions in the development of a sense of self, its meanings, and their recursive effects. Analysts seek to understand how identities connect individuals to their communities, through ethnicity, nationalism, race, gender, and other social categories. Interactions, such as the emergence or collapse of security communities, can bolster or undermine these identities. And since a sense of self often tells people who they are and what they should do, researchers also explore the impacts of these identities.

As noted in Chapter 1, constructivists use many key concepts, including the notion of identity, in disparate ways. Shifting levels of analysis adds to this diversity. For instance, those following sociology tend to focus on inter-group roles, such as "hegemon." Those influenced more by anthropology describe symbols that signify nationality, race, or gender at the local level. Cultural studies scholars shift to a macro-level when they point to distinct civilizations, religions, or ideologies as the basis for collective identities, such as "Islamic," "Christian," "democratic," or "civilized." Social psychologists disaggregate these macro-phenomena to explore how individuals adopt or reject specific self-understandings.

These approaches grant varying degrees of agency in their claims that identities need to be secured (for psychological or discursive reasons). As a result, they offer contrasting—though not necessarily incompatible—explanations for how threats to those identities create insecurities. Those starting from a structural perspective concentrate on how discourses or institutional context create and impose (often unflattering) labels on individuals and groups. Agency-oriented approaches assume that individuals, at least to some degree, instigate their roles and select among desirable characteristics or symbolic representations.

To tease out the implications of these ontological tensions, we contrast a representational approach with that of social identity theory. While we acknowledge their epistemological differences, we focus on demonstrating complementarities between these post-positivist and positivist forms of constructivism. In particular, we stress that the ontology of mutual constitution leads to the need for process-oriented methodologies that capture the inherent fluidity of identities. We also discuss some of the resulting problems of treating identities as variables along with some strategies, such as sequencing, for addressing this core methodological dispute between constructivists.

## Structure Constituting Agency

In their treatment of the state as the primary actor in world politics, mainstream IR scholars often implicitly deny the variability of identity by treating sovereignty as a defining feature of states in a system based on anarchy. At most, they relegate questions of identity to the study of nationalism in domestic societies, and hence separate IR from the subfield of comparative politics. Traditional Marxists also set aside identity issues, because they treat nationalism as an ideology of the bourgeoisie, a transnational class which controls the state. Race or gender may influence class-consciousness but, in contrast to class, neither is treated as a fundamental building block.

This theoretical position also privileges classes over nation-states as primary actors.

Constructivists challenge the static nature of these assumptions by recognizing that people have the potential to destabilize even deeply institutionalized meanings, such as sovereignty (Biersteker and Weber, eds. 1996). Post-positivists prefer the term "representations" to signify these intersubjective understandings, whereas positivists tend to use the term "norms." While these are not simply semantic differences, we find significant commonalities, including research that reveals the dynamics of contestation over meanings. Both approaches agree that meanings vary but disagree over whether to call them variables.

*Norms/Representations*

Across epistemologies, constructivists acknowledge that the identity of states as corporate actors has neither a universal nor a fixed meaning. Many scholars point out that, rather than being a characteristic or possession, statehood emanates from external recognition of sovereignty by other states. Jackson's (1990) work on "quasi-states," for example, claims that the international system defines rules for statehood. In particular, he argues that the decolonization process granted "juridical sovereignty" to former colonies based on the existence of certain basic organizational features of government, rather than any correspondence between geography and nationalism. Such standards reappear, through their absence, in characterizations of "failed" states. Grovogui (1996) concurs with the general claim that norms of sovereignty set up standards of "civilized" government that constitute decolonized states, but he points out that these norms limited the options of liberation movements. Characterizing Europe as "but a province of the world," he also claims that post-Renaissance international legal thinkers who theorized sovereignty did not recognize their intellectual debts to non-European contemporaries (Grovogui 2006).

Researching the sources and evolving meanings of sovereignty requires disentangling the commonplace equation of it with nationalism. Barkin and Cronin (1994) dissect the term "nation-state" into two ideal types of authority, suggesting that the legitimacy of states rests on territorial control, whereas nations rely on "communities of sentiment." In practice, nation-states rely on both types of authority, but the degree of overlap between state and nation in any particular instance depends on actions. By surveying the widespread use over the centuries of mass expulsions of religious minorities, ethnic cleansing, genocide, and other "homogenizing" practices, Rae (2002) underscores the difficulties that leaders face when they seek to maintain their legitimacy by creating clear geographical boundaries around nations. This tension between territorial and cultural authority has evolved historically, producing significant variation in the practice of sovereignty and the nature of the international system (see Chapter 2; also see Philpott 2001).

Defining statehood in terms of sovereignty, particularly through international law, shifts the debate away from nationalism to the ways in which norms and practices at the system-level, such as acceptance into the United Nations, can constitute state identities. The question, then, is what it means for a state to have an identity if it is not based (inherently or solely) on nationalism. Rejecting nationalism's foundational role also requires scholars to find links between "external" (or systemic) and "internal" (or domestic) sources of identity, other than (or in addition to) the strategies of cultural homogenization that Rae stresses.

Positivist-leaning studies focus on the content of those norms, concentrating on their role-defining properties. Bukovansky (1997) argues that "identity principles" create roles for states through the rules that govern their interactions. In certain circumstances, furthermore, these international principles strengthen the domestic legitimacy of the regime and lead to consistency in foreign policy. In the early days of independence, for example, in the United States leaders sought to define new post-colonial relationships with both Britain and France through existing European rules about trade and warfare. Neutrality as a role bridged internal and external sources of legitimate statehood, because neutral rights required recognition from other states as well as incorporation into the domestic legal system. Such internalized roles create stable identities by establishing consensus over fundamental political principles.

Post-positivists are more concerned with the imposition of identities through dominant representations. Extending Said's (1978; also see Chapter 3) analysis of colonial discourse, Doty (1996) juxtaposes images and metaphors to illustrate the opposition of a white, civilized, reasonable "West" to the dark, childlike, emotional, colonized populations in Kenya and the Philippines that was common among policy-makers in Britain and the United States. Classificatory schemes during the Cold War labeled the United States "good" and the Soviet Union "evil," but the Philippines "irrational," resulting in particular forms of intervention, counter-insurgency warfare, and foreign aid. This categorization process defines the identities of actors by positioning subjects (the actors) and objects (those acted upon). The resulting relationships tend to be hierarchical, although they can be neutral or complementary (Todorov 1984).

Roles and representations reflect and reinforce (or "naturalize") dominant power relationships to a point where they appear to be the only valid worldviews. Indeed, only some policies are even conceivable. As a result, people act in ways that are shaped, but not determined, by these identities. For example, states gain or lose legitimacy based on whether they abide by international norms. Those that conform to dominant practices remain free from intervention, but interference in "aberrant" ones may be deemed legitimate by a putative international community (Weber 1995; Finnemore 2003). Similarly, popular labels such as "rogue state" identify those that fail to follow international (or US-imposed) norms, while "failed" states are those without a functioning central government. Both terms grant permission for intervention, and such intervention reinforces the status of those deemed "civilized" and "successful."

Identity formation is never automatic or permanent; it always retains a contingent and temporary quality. The processes of articulation and interpellation contain inherent tensions and contradictions. For example, Said denaturalized Orientalism by showing that some of its characteristics exhibited inconsistencies, such as claims that people in the Middle East were both dangerous and naïve. This challenge should come as no surprise, since Said lived as a Christian Palestinian in both the Middle East and the West, aware of his own liminal, border-crossing identities. Similarly, Doty points out that painting a picture of colonized people as child-like assumes they cannot govern themselves and need to mature into full-fledged subjects, yet this sets the stage for demands for independence. To the extent that specific articulations of threats, or subject positions, are sheltered from or survive despite contestation, they demonstrate the power of elite discourses in "fixing" group identities.

### Stability/Fluidity

Constructivists agree in principle that identities are inherently contestable but remain at odds over when to treat these social constructions as relatively fixed. The terminology of representations tends to signal the view that identities are too unsettled and overlapping to be treated as variables. However, not all researchers who adopt the terminology of roles or norms treat identities as stable or accept the notion of variables. Our response is empirically oriented: Some identities, in certain circumstances, may be more stable than others; some may be more inclusive than others; and some may be more hierarchical than others. Research should focus on the processes of identity construction that lead to this variability, rather than staking out an epistemological position that relies on inflexible assumptions of *either* stasis *or* fluidity.

Identities do not automatically become naturalized nor do they necessarily rely upon simple dichotomies between subjects and objects. Neumann (1996, 2004), for instance, probes the tensions within Russian/Soviet identity, which he sees as the product of constant negotiation over its relationship with Europe, especially since the French Revolution called into question monarchical rule. He rejects the assumption that the state (or key leaders) selects an identity to impose on its own society or other regions of the world. Identities can be contradictory and overlapping, and are certainly contested. Religion and class are just two of the dimensions along which Russian elites consistently divide.

Similarly, Russian/Soviet views of Europe were not monolithic, though Neumann argues that the relationship to "the West" provides the primary focal point, or "deep structure," around which all internal debates about identity revolve. (Studies of Soviet leadership during the Cold War also described the recurring theme of insecurity and inferiority in relation to the West, during both Tsarist and Bolshevik eras.) Sides often shifted over whether to Westernize, destabilizing any particular representation of Europe and producing sporadic policy reversals. The growth of US power in the aftermath of World War II undermined the equation of Europe and the West. This led to rethinking about the relationship between states and classes that preceded Gorbachev. Neumann's analysis of the Russia case thus challenges simple dichotomies between colonizers and colonized, or subjects and objects, because he shows elites actively contesting identities in reference to a dominant image of the West.

Rather than crafting a narrative storyline, Neumann provides evidence of fluid identities by documenting contestation over possible alternatives. Using genealogy, he recommends starting with a relatively comprehensive and largely inductive sweep of texts, focusing on moral judgments about relationships (1996: 2-3). Then he tracks when new ideas appear in books, journals, newspapers, and other media sources, and their subsequent movements between the margins and the center of debates. The speed of these shifts may vary, creating or closing discursive opportunities. Novelty is no recipe for success, he claims.

By shifting attention toward the meanings that underlie representations and roles, Neumann reminds analysts that notions such as rights or neutrality are predicated on discourses of inclusion and exclusion. For instance, Bukovansky's study presumes a particular relationship between the United States and Europe, within which states negotiate neutrality rights and other identity principles. Her work also reminds researchers that, while international institutions establish rules that define statehood, leaders or bureaucrats make decisions that either follow or break those rules. Neumann's focus on texts recognizes that individual leaders may be embedded in social structures, but they retain less choice and therefore less responsibility for specific policies.

Others seek to retain, or regain, some sense of accountability within a textual approach. For example, in his study of US foreign policy, Campbell (1998a) questions the self-evident quality of persistent references to democracy in policy memos and treaties in order to expose discrepancies embedded in the language of the powerful. Pointing to the articulation of alternative identities, he denaturalizes this history by challenging implicit meta-narratives and creating an alternative storyline, from European encounters with Amerindians through the post-Cold War era. In his subsequent work on Bosnia, Campbell (1998b) argues that NATO and the UN supported the creation of cultural enclaves by hardliners who articulated an exclusivist understanding of ethnicity and religion, resulting in the infamous policy of "ethnic cleansing." As a result, it became difficult for other Bosnians to maintain multicultural traditions.

These are not *essential* identities, even though they are fixed at a particular historical moment. Nor will such entrenched exclusionary identities *always* trump alternative multicultural ones. No single set of identities necessarily prevails, as Wilmer (2002) shows in her ethnographic exploration of diverse voices in the former Yugoslavia. Similarly, in his study of the evolution of pan-Arabism, Barnett (1998) sees transnational and state identities coexisting, although not necessarily comfortably. Through a process of "dialogue," he argues, multiple identities can overlap and influence each other. This flowing of identities across borders in the Middle East and the Balkans illustrates some of the transnational cultural processes that anthropologist Appadurai (1996) labels "ethnoscapes." Diasporas, even more obviously than cross-border dialogues, carry practices across territories, potentially forcing states to articulate identities which span competing national or ethnic claims. Countries of immigration, such as Australia and Canada, for instance, routinely revise their multiculturalism policies in an attempt to mute the social conflicts that can result from cultural differences.

### Variability

As post-positivists frequently point out in their critiques of studies focusing on international norms, a state-centric view of identity can mask complex global-local connections that highlight the mutability of identities. However, calling into question whether identities have any boundaries raises an even more basic question: does the concept of identity then lose its analytical value? As Brubaker and Cooper provocatively proclaim, "If identity is everywhere, it is nowhere" (2000: 1). In response, we follow Goff and Dunn (2004a: 3-4), who advocate unpacking and repacking the component processes surrounding identity in order to understand how they are interrelated and when they reinforce each other.

To pursue this unpacking and repacking empirically, analysts need to establish a baseline against which to compare identities. Some may think of time or location as variables in contrasting discourses at "T1" to those at "T2" or in "place A" and "place B." Those seeking to denaturalize identities also demonstrate that alternative understandings are possible using historical or cross-case comparisons. With either strategy, researchers must be careful not to treat any particular period as the absolute or objective foundation of a group's identity, because others can always put forth alternative interpretations or reach back further into the past (as we saw with the demarcation of historical periods in Chapter 2). After establishing a baseline, analysts can describe sources and forms of identity using process-sensitive techniques, such as genealogy and narrative, which draw attention to how people think about the characteristics, roles, status, and functions that comprise group identities.

Where to cut into this research depends, in part, on whether the focus is on stability or fluidity. One might start by looking at the origins of strong self-conceptions and then concentrate on how they resist subsequent challenges. Or one might contrast one identity with contemporaneous ones in order to track their trajectories over time. None of these strategies are inherently better or worse than the others. Some are well-suited to probing the tensions between external and internal (or transnational) components of identity, others to parsing the significance of alternative internal (or external) factors.

However, particularly for those who explore the recursive effects of identities, documentation can become problematic. If researchers use foreign policies as evidence of state identities, they risk tautology if they claim that identities contribute to the selection of those same policies. One strategy (advocated in Klotz 2006) is to select another issue-area that complements traditional foreign policy issues like war and trade. Immigration policy in particular cuts to the core of a state's identification of "us" and "them." For non-state actors, similar core issues may concern women's rights, class benefits, or the practice of religious beliefs within their own organizations, not solely as policies that they advocate for others at the local, national, or global levels. The goal is to grasp how changes in identity matter by tracing roles and characteristics through discourse on a critical policy issue. The challenge is to select evidence that honors the simultaneity of *mutual* constitution without simply conflating structure and agency.

All of these strategies provide insights into the overarching question of which processes enable certain identities to take hold. But they say less about how proponents of representations bolster particular frames or norms. Since the stabilization of identities requires constant vigilance, we turn to agent-oriented approaches to questions of identity.

## Agency Constituting Structure

Constructivists agree broadly that identity is based on a division between "us" and "them." In the language of psychology, social identity theorists examine how categorization creates an "in-group" that subordinates an "out-group." Using the language of alterity, followers of Foucault argue that subjects produce representations that objectify an "Other" that lacks the capacity to rewrite these discourses. Across their theoretical and terminological differences, constructivists agree that identities are constituted through comparisons, which researchers describe and interpret. Both social identity and representational approaches also claim that comparison creates inherent hierarchies.

Where these approaches diverge is over who inscribes these comparisons and the extent to which they get institutionalized. Sometimes individuals can choose definitions for themselves (and for the states on whose behalf they may speak), but under certain circumstances, that definition may impose identities upon others. Representational theorists, drawing especially on Althusser and

Hall (see Suggested Readings), posit that elites construct difference through the "articulation" of particular identities, into which
they "interpellate" other people to provide legitimacy for their
own dominance. This framework places agency in one group's
ability to project identities onto others. In contrast, psychologists
conceptualize these social processes in terms of categorization and
selection, placing agency in the individual.

### Categorization/Articulation

Individuals and groups value certain characteristics over others.
People make sense of the world by noticing differences, such as how
others celebrate holidays (nationality), read newspapers (language),
attend meetings (political affiliation), cut their hair (gender, race)
and worship (religion)—to list just a few of the routine practices
that comprise identity discourses. Often people do not pay attention
or accord special significance to such ordinary tasks until they see
others doing them differently, as may happen when immigrants
move into a neighborhood.

Social identity theorists explore how and why individuals convert
their perceptions of difference into categories that define groups
(Larson and Shevchenko 2003; also see Monroe et al. 2000). This
leads to the second step: identification with a particular group.
People recognize that they belong to certain social categories
but not others, what are known as "in-groups" and "out-groups."
Finally, people attribute value to this "we" feeling by contrasting
themselves to those others, usually according prestige and status to
the most valued components of identity. Comparisons might lead
to negative or neutral evaluations, but people tend to exaggerate
both the homogeneity of an in-group and negative judgments about
their corresponding out-groups. As a result, stereotypes become
quite common.

To understand how self-perceptions, such as stereotypes, influence cognition and behavior, social psychologists often describe
these mental images as schemata, comparable to the frames of social
movement theory. Both schemas and frames provide stable and coherent guidelines for action, based primarily upon what actors say

in their own words. Framing concentrates on group cohesion and policy prescriptions, while schemas focus on how people categorize and rank themselves in relation to other groups. (Some sociologists use the term schema rather than frame. To avoid confusion, we refer to schemas for individuals and frames for groups.) Framing meshes well with causal stories of mobilization, whereas social identity theory assesses individual status within a group. As a result, both incorporate an element of identity affirmation in their evaluations of success and failure. Indeed, combining the two approaches would lead us to expect that framing would be most successful when its policy prescriptions reinforce in-group identities.

Applied to international relations, this social-psychological approach concentrates on an individual's self-perceptions in relation to others, as evident, for instance, in the language of status and prestige through which leaders promote particular policies. Following the three stages of identity formation, analysts look for the categories that groups use for self-understanding and comparison, including stereotypes, and then trace how these get translated into status and ranking, through favoritism and other such practices. For example, during the Cold War, US and Soviet elites compared themselves to each other on multiple dimensions. They drew on disparities in military power, economic productivity, technological innovation, and human rights, to create prejudiced images of each other, exemplified by Ronald Reagan's famous comments about the "evil empire."

Although it focuses on individuals, social identity theory acknowledges that people live in broader contexts, particularly when identities are posited as a factor in policy choices. For instance, some form of historiography is essential for multi-causal explanations in which psychological approaches offer specific individual motivations for (or mechanisms of) change. Applied to political leaders, social identity theory also relies on prior understandings of the bureaucratic context which gives them authority to make policy choices (which, presumably, reaffirm desirable identities) on behalf of a group, such as the state (or nation or class). Usually analysts presume that leaders speak on behalf of these groups, but certainly in-fighting over the definition of group identities, or other dimensions of conflict, may warrant further investigation of, say, the political campaigns or bureaucratic maneuverings that put those leaders into power in the first place.

A representational approach, in contrast, places these issues of context at the center of analysis, rather than at the margins. Hopf (2002), for example, treats the statements of Soviet/Russian leaders as representative of wider societal discourses and therefore looks primarily at everyday articulations of these identities. Modifying ethnographic precepts for historical research, he reads popular culture, primarily novels and magazines, to recreate the social context in which leaders made decisions, noting contestations over class in 1955 and nationality in 1999. After mapping dominant representations in each era, Hopf traces these tropes and images to the level of foreign policy choices. Much like practitioners of historical narrative, he seeks to document the socio-historical background within which specific identities form. Drawing on evidence from organizational documents and leaders' speeches, he clusters articulations of group identities, such as "New Soviet Man." But rather than offering a causal storyline that locates individual motivations for particular policy choices, he concentrates on categorizing the societal discourses that make particular foreign policies conceivable.

What is missing from this representational approach, then, is an explanation for why certain individuals, particularly national leaders, reflect one or another of these multiple societal identities. Social identity theory offers a complementary approach, since it focuses primarily on the relationship between individuals, such as key leaders, and their social contexts. This leads to the question of how and why individuals select, or "interpellate," a particular set of identities when multiple ones are available.

## Selection/Interpellation

The content of a schema or representation derives from the context in which individuals live. Both psychological and representational approaches concentrate on processes of labeling to understand how people select from, or are interpellated into, a range of possible identifications. For those speaking the language of alterity, identity labels derive from discursive oppositions, such as those reiterated in narratives of nationalism and their tropes of insecurity. The act of challenging dichotomies ("deconstruction") opens space for alternate articulations of identity. (Whether those alternatives rely on dichotomies of their own is a point of further debate among representational theorists.) Social identity theory focuses less on text and more on choice. The mechanism for social psychologists is the individual need for positive associations and memberships in higher status groups, whereas representation theorists stress socialization.

Given that social identity theory proposes that people desire to be members of positively valued groups, several choices are open to those who perceive themselves to be in low status groups (Larson and Shevchenko 2003: 79). Individuals may try to move into a higher status group ("social mobility"). Alternatively, remaining as members of the lower status group, they may seek to improve their collective ranking by competing against higher status groups ("social competition"). Or they may attempt to redefine the criteria for status ("social creativity"). These alternatives assume a high degree of autonomy at the level of the individual. When analysis moves to the level of states, these choices can readily be converted into hypotheses about national leaders that link identity to foreign policy. Declining international status as a result of technological inferiority, for instance, creates conditions conducive to identity change. But choices depend on the permeability of group boundaries. Since foreign-policy decision-makers rarely have the option of joining another national group (short of exile or treason), international competition and creative rewriting of status criteria are more likely scenarios.

Illustrating the application of social identity theory in the Soviet case, Larson and Shevchenko suggest that Gorbachev and his key advisors adopted the social creativity option in the 1980s, following the failure of military competition during the peak of the Cold War. These leaders hoped that "a new global mission" in a redefined international order would strengthen the country's status as a great power in a time of severe economic constraints, while also preserving its "national identity" (Larson and Shevchenko 2003: 78). Alternative materialist and ideational analyses, they claim, cannot adequately explain why Gorbachev opted for the notion of a "common European home" in particular, rather than more conventional or less-risky options.

This "New Thinking" overturned so many fundamental features of Soviet policy thinking that, in Larson and Shevchenko's view, it signaled a change in identity. A humanitarian universalist streak incorporated arms control and human rights ideals circulating among European social democrats and in trans-Atlantic networks, thus breaking down the boundaries between in-groups and out-groups. The world was no longer divided between capitalists and communists; conflict between the superpowers was not inevitable. Yet, New Thinking still drew on the Soviet past, including a persistent comparison between Russia and Europe, rather than Asia, and skepticism about liberal individualism. Gorbachev also remained comfortable with the tradition of centralized decision-making that gave him authority to speak on behalf of the whole country in defining its identity.

Larson and Shevchenko explain Soviet identity change based on the decline of international standing and the selection of a strategy that boosted status at a lower material cost. Combining Neumann's and Hopf's documentation of competing domestic Soviet/Russian identities with Larson and Shevchenko's framework for how leaders choose from this array provides basic building blocks for analyzing the connections between individual and group (including state) identities. But the emphasis is on how individuals reflect societal discourses. It leaves unanswered questions about when leaders and their policies transform those societal discourses. For instance, while Hopf documents a shift in societal identities evident between 1955 and 1999, he cannot explain it with his ethnographic methods.

The notion of interpellation explores this dimension of the constitutive relationship between leaders and societies. For example, in her study of foreign policy discourses during the 1962 Cuban Missile Crisis, Weldes (1999) reveals conceptions of global leadership that mirror the sort that Larson and Shevchenko say Gorbachev sought to reclaim for the Soviet Union in the late 1980s. Viewed through a prism of rivalry, US leaders interpreted the Soviet installation of missiles in Cuba as a "crisis" because it challenged the demarcation of spheres of influence, a fundamental component of its leadership. By labeling the situation a crisis, only certain responses could then be conceived as possible, virtually eliminating other options from the start. As with all interpretations, these representations cannot be verified as "true," but analysts can confirm whether previously inconceivable policies do indeed become possible. Once identity discourse shifts, so should the options subsequently debated by decision-makers. Indeed, Weldes shows that those who had initially suggested tolerating the missiles in Cuba quickly fell silent. Thus, she can pinpoint the types of actions legitimized by particular identities.

Interpellation refers to the process through which people accept or adopt an identity articulated by elites. Publics are "hailed" into specific identities through the reiteration of characteristics of selves and others. People presumably acquiesce to, or actively embrace, representations when they recognize themselves in these tropes. Drawing on cultural references and common vocabulary, elites try to speak in a language that resonates with their audiences. For example, Weldes demonstrates that US elites during the Cuban Missile Crisis contrasted their own peaceful intentions with the apparent duplicity and aggressiveness of Soviet actions. Using practices that touched individuals in their daily lives, such as emergency drills in schools to train students how to protect themselves in the event of nuclear attack and public service announcements that encouraged people to stockpile food, politicians communicated their interpretation of the threat. Similarly, Dunn (2003) demonstrates how views of war in the Congo that replicate images from Conrad's *The Heart of Darkness* sound familiar and accurate to people who know nothing about Africa. The participant-observations discussed in Chapter 2 further explain such constitutive effects of language at the individual level.

Leaders must constantly reproduce these tropes and metaphors because alternative identities are always possible. While one might analyze this as strategic articulation of collective goals, as in framing, Campbell (1998a) conceives of it as a performance that constitutes state identity through inscriptions of dangers. Either way, leaders have some control over this "public" discourse through state institutions, which can marginalize alternative articulations of identity. For instance, as Neumann (1996: 4) points out, censorship enables leaders to circumscribe debate at the same time that they participate in it. Because leaders are stage managers, not simply actors, analysts should not be surprised that they tend to succeed in imposing identities. And these become the social environments out of which the next generation of leaders emerges, creating continuity and stability in the articulation of identities over time.

In applying the notion of interpellation, however, researchers should not simply equate "publics" with "societies." Foreign-policy makers might treat bureaucrats from other ministries, rather than mass publics, as audiences that need to be hailed. Certainly the US Congress precludes easy categorization. That Gorbachev's rise shifted the US view of the Soviet Union signals even more potential publics, such as allies and international organizations. Others include a transnational dimension as well. For example, Barnett (1998) emphasizes variation in the external context within which Arab leaders articulate identities. The role of sovereign state, for instance, is more formal and constraining than informal roles that derive from a shared regional history of anti-colonial mobilization. In some states, external and internal dimensions converge into nationalism, whereas other states are more strongly influenced by transnational pan-Arab solidarity.

Inevitably, researchers encounter a wide array of possible identities (e.g., the diverse contributions in Goff and Dunn 2004b). Multiple discourses can "hail" people into complex and competing identities, possibly leading to conflicting self-understandings. For individuals, psychologists commonly call this an identity crisis. Analogously, domestic regimes may have a legitimacy crisis when competing identities cannot be reconciled. Indeed, the most relevant Other may be a person's or a country's past. Subordination can occur within groups as well as between them. Policy-makers in the European Union, for instance, confront such complexity on a regular basis. Wiener (1998), Checkel (1999), and Koslowski (2000) all point out that citizenship rights intersect debates over constitutions, expansion, and identity.

The potential for multiple publics may ultimately be more of a methodological issue than a conceptual problem. Questions of audience guide researchers to public rather than private expressions of identity. (Of course feminists fundamentally challenge this distinction between public and private.) For instance, speeches rather than confidential diplomatic cables capture the performative aspects inherent in public pronouncements. With evidence of these multiple identities in hand, analysts can then turn to the question of the relationship between them.

## Sequencing

The studies that we have surveyed here lay out many possible paths for the constitution of identities. Bukovansky and Weldes suggest interstate interaction. Barnett and Larson and Shevchenko wrestle with transnational diffusion. Hopf and Neumann concentrate on domestic contestation. Despite their terminological differences, all show how collectivities, such as the state, can have identities. Yet they risk talking past each other, because it is not always clear whether they aim to understand identity formation as an outcome (or "dependent variable"), to assess their effects (as "independent variables"), or some recursive combination of the two (which might preclude the differentiation between independent and dependent variables).

The notion of "path dependence" helps to untangle the recursive dynamics of mutual constitution, including the significance of identities. Mechanisms of "positive feedback," rather than historical determinism or sunk costs, explain why certain practices become institutionalized into "paths" where only some policy choices are conceivable (Pierson 2004; also see Cederman 1997). Notably, the timing and sequence of these reinforcing effects matter greatly for sorting out when certain practices (or by extension, meanings of identity) prevail. Path dependency arguments thus complement genealogies in that they seek to explain the significance of critical junctures. Yet their use of rival interest-based explanations points to one of the most fundamental tensions within constructivism: how to interpret the material dimension of reality. This leads analysts to explore the relationship between interests and identities.

Most constructivists treat interests as social constructions, much like identities. For example, Weldes (1999) uses "identity," "interests," and "the security imaginary" interchangeably, with each influencing the others through self-reinforcing processes of articulation and interpellation. Teasing these apart reveals an implicit sequential relationship. Identities connote subject positions which empower certain speakers to define collective interests. Only goals or priorities compatible with those identities, such as removing Soviet missiles from Cuba, will be a conceivable basis for selecting policies, such as the choice between an airstrike and a blockade. Identities and interests may not be separate variables, but they may be sufficiently distinguishable in their discursive content to warrant more precise differentiation, particularly in their potential effects. Only then can analysts explore the possibility of interests serving as a source of identities, which offers one explanation for the multiplicity and fluidity of (conflicting or overlapping) identities.

Some constructivists retain the notion that interests derive from material rather than ideational sources. For example, Abdelal (2001) sharply differentiates between material interests and socially constructed identities. Identity, in his study of the divergent economic trajectories of post-Soviet states, becomes the *intervening* variable between interests and policy outcomes. Societal groups, and hence governments, draw on cross-nationally variable notions of identity, but they face similar structural economic constraints. Consequently, they advocate different policies. To explain why nationalists are more willing than industrialists to accept economic sacrifices, Abdelal adopts a rationalist framework that stresses costs and benefits.

But a stark distinction between constructed identities and material interests also has limitations. By equating identity with nationalism, Abdelal reduces it to coalition dynamics, as he assesses the extent to which nationalists ally with industrialists and communists. In contrast, Neumann's (1996) alterity approach suggests that a discourse of Russia-as-the-Other may have constituted each of these interest groups. Researchers could modify Abdelal's rationalist framework with Larson and Shevchenko's (2003) social identity theory to incorporate status as a social benefit (and its loss as a cost). Weldes cautions, though, that actions not taken were not necessarily more costly; they may simply not have been articulated as possible.

These differences between Abdelal, on the one hand, and Weldes and Neumann, on the other, highlight some of the difficulties in disentangling the relationship between identities and interests. Although both are the outcomes of constitutive processes, researchers should not conflate the two. Reliance on materialist and rationalist alternative frameworks also overlooks some key dynamics of social construction. Attention to the timing and sequence, as suggested by the notion of path dependency, offers one avenue for disentangling the complex interactions between identities and interests.

## Implications

Identities become institutionalized and thus part of the context within which people act. Some identities complement or reinforce while others undermine or contradict each other. Because identities are potentially malleable rather than static, people can alter them. Identities, therefore, are somewhere between "deep structure" and "free-floating signifier," in Neumann's (2004) terminology. To tease apart some of this complexity and potential inconsistency, we juxtaposed research strategies from both ends of the epistemological spectrum. Certainly social psychology and representation differ over whether to emphasize the self-construction of identity within a social context or the discursive imposition of identity in a historical context. Yet both approaches suggest comparable or complementary explanations for how and why identities change. Clarification and elaboration of these claims would provide a wider range of methodological tools for constructivist research on identity issues.

Because the works we have assessed here focus on states and foreign policy, we have bracketed a number of other identity-based research agendas that deserve further exploration. For instance, by concentrating on sovereignty rather than nationalism, we grappled with the question of how to conceptualize "state identity" rather than looking at social movements or other non-actors. To some extent our selections reinforce the separation of IR from comparative politics. This reifies the state, a move we do not generally endorse. Particularly at a time when studies of "globalization" draw attention to the impacts of international dynamics on domestic processes, we encourage greater attention to contestation over all identities.

Our focus on the state should not be interpreted as an ontological claim about the primacy of the state in IR theory. It is an example of the issues involved in any research that takes socially constructed collectivities, rather than individuals, as the unit of analysis. We encourage elaboration of propositions from social psychology and representation to bridge agency and structure in other domestic and transnational settings (e.g., Monroe et al. 2000; Cederman and Daase 2003). In some circumstances, it may be useful to apply social psychological approaches to corporate actors, such as states or non-governmental organizations, through the use of analogy and metaphor. At other times, it may be more appropriate to disaggregate these collectives into leaders and their constituents.

Regardless of whether researchers concentrate on individual or collective agency, constructivists need to denaturalize the conflation of identities and interests. Temporal sequencing is only one methodological tool at our disposal to pursue these lines of research, and like all techniques, it has its strengths and weaknesses. Rival explanations, especially those based on material interests or rational calculations of costs and benefits help analysts to tease out specific claims about identities. But these build on contested assumptions about a material basis for interests and objective calculations of costs and benefits. These too need to be placed under constructivist scrutiny, a task we turn to in the next chapter.

# Chapter Five

# Interests

Many constructivists treat the state as a corporate actor comprised of relatively stable identities and institutions. Consequently, "national interests" are what states (or their leaders, on behalf of the collective) want or need. Analysts of foreign policy often treat these interests as the basis for decisions that result from leaders evaluating, and balancing a variety of implicit and explicit, short-term and long-term strategic, economic, and ethical concerns. Even during times of structural stability, such as the Cold War, the state is driven by diverse and mutable concerns (e.g., Wolfers 1962). Distributions of military power alone do not determine whether leaders will fight or trade, build more weapons or negotiate reductions, or demonstrate strength through military preponderance or the vibrance of their democratic institutions.

Constructivists thus challenge the common assumption in IR (among most Realists, Liberals, and Marxists) that interests derive (in one way or another) from material sources. Identities underpin interests. Military measures may be used to meet external threats, but the definition of who or what must be protected determines the appropriateness or efficacy of those weapons systems. Positing "survival" as the most basic interest presumes a Self to be preserved. Those constructivists particularly concerned to tap the potential for social change examine how non-state actors seek to redefine state interests, because the terms of legitimacy define survival. Those who examine alliances point out that shared identity expands the boundaries of the Self and increases the costs that states may be willing to bear to achieve collective security. These issues lead researchers to explore the origins of interests in identities, institutions, and interactions.

To disentangle this complex relationship between "who we are" and "what we want," we contrast two types of studies of interest transformation. First, we tackle the issue of levels of analysis by surveying arguments that use comparative case studies to differentiate international, domestic, and transnational influences, primarily focusing on state leaders. Since these studies suggest a range of potential processes, we then concentrate on those scholars who explore communication and negotiation as two mechanisms that can change interests. This focus on speech as action brings us back to debates over rationality. But, we argue, unresolved issues of intentionality, rather than rationality, are at the center of abiding divisions among constructivists.

## Selecting Comparisons

Like identities, interests are neither self-evident nor static; their formation is a process that needs to be explained. Conceptualizing interests as the product of interactions and institutionalized identities presumes intersubjective content. Therefore, constructivists reject the juxtaposition of altruistic and instrumental motivations as a misleading separation between norms and interests. Seeking evidence that people or states act beyond narrow self-interest is insufficient, not least because any action can (at least after the fact) be reduced to interest-based motivations. The challenge is to come up with research designs that demonstrate the intersubjective dimension of interests as well as refute conventional materialist conceptualizations. (We are concentrating here on only one dimension of mutual constitution. Norms, as components of structure, are themselves shaped by prior understandings of interest, as discussed in Chapter 2.)

Comparative case studies are the most common tool that constructivists use to untangle this constitutive dimension. Clearly, the rationale for case selection is crucial, because emphasis on particular combinations of similarities and differences can justify alternative case studies (George and McKeown 1985; Ragin 1994; Odell 2001; George and Bennett 2005). Researchers also frequently use hypothetical scenarios as foils, often deductively deriving these from alternative explanations. (Counterfactuals have their own advantages and limitations. See Fearon 1991; Tetlock and Belkin 1996.) The language of causality and the logic of variables prevail in these studies, which hold certain factors (relatively) constant through the selection of cases, but such terminology is not required. Even a single case implies comparison, since it serves as the basis for making general claims or as a way of stressing the uniqueness of particular experiences. Regardless of whether analysts privilege generalization or detail, comparisons need to avoid two potential pitfalls: complementary arguments across levels of analysis being mistaken for competing explanations, and case selection that conflates processes and outcomes.

### Levels of Analysis

Because constructivists locate the sources of interests at several levels, analysts need to differentiate complementary explanations across levels of analysis from contrasting ones at the same level of analysis. Some researchers concentrate on the international context, such as the impact of norms that diffuse through interstate interactions, international regimes, and transnational epistemic communities. Others look within the state to comprehend how foreign policy goals get selected from competing visions. These factors, operating at different levels of analysis, may offer complementary explanations, such as international norms that inform some domestic articulations of interests. Or they may serve as competing explanations, as when one analyst argues for the significance of social movements, while another contends that international organizations matter more. Appropriate case selection depends on how the researcher sets up the question.

Since one of constructivism's main points is that the international system is comprised of social structures, one of its basic claims is that this ideational context creates states as actors (with identities and interests). This view goes beyond conventional studies of regimes, which stress behavioral compliance; international organizations are more than arenas in which actors learn new norms (see Chapter 2). As independent actors who actively promote norms, these international organizations can have a deeper constitutive impact on states. For example, Finnemore (1996) argues that sometimes international organizations "teach" states. She shows that UNESCO (the United Nations Educational, Scientific, and Cultural Organization) promoted a view of science that equated being a modern state with having a particular form of science policy bureaucracy. Enticed by the desire to be accepted as modern states, national leaders embraced the goal of establishing the requisite bureaucracies despite the immediate costs. This undermined the view among scientists that their research should be a transnational activity.

It is reasonable to conclude that these far-reaching impacts on both the content and form of the state can be characterized as a change in interests. The internalization of a particular understanding of science fundamentally alters policy goals, as a result of an epistemic shift about how the world works. New bureaucracies may also alter basic organizational features of the state as an actor, determining who makes decisions on behalf of the collectivity. Documenting the development of bureaucracies over time also circumvents the problem of tautology, because analysts do not infer interests from the same foreign policy outcomes that interests presumably explain.

Since Finnemore focuses on international organizations as advocates of norms, she compares their roles across policy arenas, rather than selecting states as her unit of analysis. She strengthens her claim for the pervasiveness of "teaching" as a mechanism of norm diffusion by selecting a broad array of issues, from the laws of war to poverty alleviation. Her cases describe and assess the evolution of policy thinking within international organizations. Then she traces the impact of new thinking on member states and their policies. She complements evidence from policy debates with aggregate data to confirm a correlation in the patterns of establishing science bureaucracies across states. In many cases, the resulting policies reinforce international regimes, further strengthening the socialization process.

Finnemore also refutes alternative arguments based on materialist or rationalist premises to bolster her conclusion that bureaucracies and practitioners within states would not have adopted new priorities and procedures in the absence of the diffusion of international norms. With no apparent material reward, she argues, states around the world adopted national science bureaucracies. In the case of international development norms, national elites had little incentive to promote poverty alleviation prior to World Bank initiatives. Yet developing states responded by shifting from a growth-generating approach to a welfare-oriented one. They even took up the banner of anti-poverty programs, becoming vocal advocates for this new approach in other international organizations. Similarly, instrumental arguments based on reciprocity cannot fully explain why states adopt rules for the protection of the wounded in wartime.

However, because Finnemore bases her comparisons on issue areas, she makes assumptions about the nature of the state that merit further investigation. For example, she traced the timing of the insertion of new conceptions of "science" and "development" in recipient states to show that these ideas originated outside of the state. But she leaves unresolved the question of whether to treat states as unitary actors with coherent interests, as in-fighting bureaucracies who advocate competing interests, as aggregates of domestic groups where one dominates another, or any number of alternative conceptions of the domestic arena.

This is an empirical question that can be answered by looking specifically at who takes up, or "learns," the new norms that are taught by transnational epistemic communities and international organizations. (This notion of learning complements the process of "interpellation" that we discussed in Chapter 4, raising similar questions about audience that we will not repeat here.) A more systematic comparison across recipient states shows how domestic constituencies respond to external "teaching" and weigh the various factors that determine whether diffusion will lead to internalization of these new norms and practices. Crossing these levels of analysis would provide a more complete analysis.

Comparing diverse responses to a single issue, such as racial discrimination in South Africa, probes more fully the domestic dimensions of norm diffusion and suggests some cross-national conditions for "success" or "failure." Examining the relationship between elites and broader societal forces, for instance, Klotz (1995) argues that variation in the compatibility between international and domestic racial norms explains internalization in some states, such as Zimbabwe and the United States, and resistance in others, such as Britain. She distinguishes two paths of change in state interests. Social revolution, by definition, dramatically transforms who makes policy and their basic worldviews. In Zimbabwe, new ruling elite came to power in 1980, overturning the previous Rhodesian regime's priorities. As a result, the country's policies toward South Africa shifted substantially, within the constraints of regional economic and military imbalances. However, revolutions remain fairly rare events and hardly explain most cases of interest reformulation. Incremental shifts, more typical of foreign policy-making, can also indicate fundamental rethinking. But demonstrating this empirically is more difficult.

Hypothetical scenarios built upon alternative theoretical frameworks provide additional tools for deciding what merits labeling as a change in interests, rather than less-fundamental, instrumental adaptation in strategic thinking. To counter Realist or Marxist explanations, for instance, Klotz asked why states follow human rights norms when doing so alienates an ally whose territory holds critical natural resources. In the case of US policy toward apartheid South Africa, the promotion of non-racial democracy did eventually override considerations based on immediate economic or material gains. By tracing public articulations of national interests, she pinpointed when governmental and societal actors made new arguments about apartheid, and when policy-makers' preferences shifted. Her analysis builds on a rationalist framework by demarcating a fundamental change in interests when there is evidence of a reordering of preferences. At the same time, it calls into question the presumption of the pursuit of self-interest by showing that actors may privilege ethical goals at significant (material) cost. Meanings are not simply the political equivalents of commodities that can be bought and sold as resources.

Rather than claiming that either international or domestic actors prevailed, Klotz describes the interactions between them to explain how the United States belatedly joined the growing momentum for sanctions against South Africa, even though its domestic social movements had been integrated into a transnational anti-apartheid network for decades. She illustrates just a few of the ways that individuals, societies, and international organizations factor into multi-causal explanations across levels of analysis. That shifts in US preferences resulted, in part, from public pressures generated by activists connected to a wider global movement underscores the need to consider in more depth the transnational non-governmental sources of interests. This requires a different type of case selection, one more oriented towards mechanisms that explain *how* and *why* interests changed rather than documenting that interests did change.

## *Processes*

While constructivists may agree that states get socialized into the international system, drawing attention to processes rather than outcomes paints significantly different pictures of power dynamics, capabilities, and disparities. By focusing on the evolution of norms, for example, Finnemore draws attention to structural continuities and intentional change. The notions of teaching and learning downplay power. Yet socialization inherently involves discursive inequalities. By showing that policy-makers can shift from instrumental to normative policy frames, Klotz gives greater weight to the value-laden activities of domestic and transnational social movements.

Adler (1992) unpacks agency even further in his study of super-power arms control. Indeed, his emphasis on transnational networking produces a single case study of interaction rather than a comparison of two separate foreign policies. As in Finnemore's study, the creation or strengthening of arms control bureaucracies signifies that the interests (or preference rankings) of these states changed. Delineating the sequence of key decisions is an appropriate process-tracing method for such a detailed study of diffusion and decision-making (George and Bennett 2005).

Adler distinguishes three phases in the transformation of state interests: the development of arms control ideas within the United States, the diffusion of these views into the Soviet Union, and finally the institutionalization of the arms control perspective in both states. He starts by documenting the role of scientific and political elites in the United States as advocates of new ideas and shows how their interactions brought people together into an emerging arms control epistemic community. From the onset of the Cold War, he identifies the central proponents of the new arms control concept, their institutional (or employer) base, status within the scientific community, and connections to the policy world. One of the most significant characteristics of these arms-controllers proved to be their access to key foreign policy decision-makers and the credibility of their expertise in a highly technical area. Adler claims that the ability to convince both President Kennedy and Secretary of Defense McNamara of the need for arms control marked major successes for the epistemic community in the first stage of reaching a bilateral agreement.

In the second stage, arms control ideas diffused through interaction between the United States and the Soviet Union, despite a hostile Cold War context which limited diplomatic contact. Two lines of communication enabled ideas to filter across borders. At one level, Soviet elites gained access to views expressed in public US debates. Scientists themselves also served as a cross-national link. Adler documents how Soviet officials adopted almost verbatim some of the key arguments from US scientists. Finally, in the third stage, institutionalization of these arms control ideas within both US and Soviet bureaucracies is manifest in new treaty priorities.

Concentrating on the interactions between relatively equal superpowers, however, loses sight of the more hierarchical world that Finnemore and Klotz present. International institutions and great powers create rules that significantly influence other states. States do not always incorporate norms voluntarily, through processes of education, communication, and persuasion. Sometimes coercive tactics are needed to produce compliance. For instance, Finnemore noted that the World Bank withheld aid until states adopted acceptable development policies. Some states evade even these more coercive measures, as South Africa did for decades. In other words, socialization is fraught with contention, because some actors seek to impose or instill their values.

Greater attention to resistance and contestation highlights processes that otherwise might be hidden by the silence of acquiescence. For example, only after decades of resistance to international pressures did many South African elites reevaluate apartheid practices. To explain their increasing receptivity to norms of nonracialism, Black (1999) points to the significance of international sports boycotts in particular. Preventing South African national teams from participating in world championships, he argues, both punished whites for their racist practices (including failure to field integrated teams) and delegitimized the ideology at the heart of minority-rule, ultimately corroding white morale. These measures affected politicians directly as well as indirectly, since rugby played such a strong socializing role within leadership circles. While sports sanctions did not single-handedly overthrow apartheid, individual motivations and societal desires contributed to a broad reassessment of party priorities and hence interests.

Black's and Adler's analyses underscore the need to question whose interests are at stake—to avoid implicit reification of the state. Individuals and groups who reside within or across state boundaries have overlapping, complementary, and competing goals, which may also be changed through participation in international regimes and cross-border interactions. These actors' interests may not correspond to, or coalesce into, those of states-as-actors. The existence of development specialists, anti-apartheid activists, and scientists promoting arms control illustrate that people's conceptions of their interests need not be bound by the territorial state or a narrow definition of personal gain. Constructivists contrast the principles of advocacy networks to the instrumentality of a corporation's pursuit of profit. But the nature of non-state actors needs to be a research question, not an assumption. A transnational network might operate as an interest group in a one country while acting through a loosely organized social movement or political party in another.

These possibilities underscore the need to explore more systematically why and how, or "under what general conditions," states and non-state actors redefine their interests. By tracing the spread of norms across state boundaries and into societies, analysts can better understand the processes that constitute the interests of all of these actors. Only then can we fully appreciate their potential influence on each other. Researching the interests of non-state actors requires indicators or measures of socialization beyond bureaucratization, because the interests of informal networks and social movements are more fluid than those of states. And when non-state actors do rely heavily on bureaucracies, such as professional human rights monitoring organizations or corporations, analysts need to delve into their component groups and individuals, which will differ from the domestic constituents of states.

Accessing sufficient information to do detailed research on interest formation can be a challenge. Particularly in the realm of foreign policy, tracing individual choices requires documents that often remain secret. Even when policy-makers such as Robert McNamara, who played a critical role both in arms control as Secretary of Defense and in development as President of the World Bank, are forthcoming with interviews and autobiographies, they may have strong personal incentives to rewrite history. These are not problems unique to states, however. Corporations are often quite closed when it comes to information that might benefit their competitors, while social activists often try to keep any less-than-principled behavior out of the limelight.

Public discourse, alternatively, may provide better evidence for the articulation of interests because it reveals normative rationales for policy. Unlike bureaucratization, it necessarily conceptualizes language as action, not simply as evidence, leading scholars to think more systematically about processes of communication. But it lacks the capacity to expose individual cognition, the deepest level of socialization. For that, researchers may be better off studying language through participant-observation (Chapter 2) or testing predictions built on the personal motivations posited by social identity theory (Chapter 4). In the next section, we explore in more detail these competing claims about mechanisms of change and appropriate methodologies to capture evidence of processes.

## Contrasting Interactions

Constructivism posits a wide range of processes that may change the basic nature of states as actors, as well as their specific goals and policy choices. Technical experts may persuade key decision-makers to adopt new priorities or to mandate the establishment of new agencies, for example, or social movements may exert normative pressure through frames that shame politicians and mobilize voters. Although they take different forms, all of these practices require communication, leading Müller to conclude that "international politics consists predominantly of actions that take the form of language" (2001: 161). The methodological challenge for some scholars is to separate evidence of processes of interest formation from instrumental bargaining between actors with stable interests.

Reflecting debates within speech act theory (see Suggested Readings), constructivist research tends to follow one of two directions. One group, drawing on communicative action theory, concentrates on the public exchange of ideas. The other group sees greater power inequalities in these exchanges, which they characterize as language games. Both approaches wrestle with—but do not resolve—tensions about agents' rationality.

### *Communicative Action*

Communicative and strategic action are two types of speech that are manifest in diplomatic language (Müller 2001, 2004; based on Habermas, see Suggested Readings). Consistent with a rationalist conception of utility maximization, strategic action "concerns itself with the realization of self-interest by means of influence on objects, be these things or persons" (Müller, 2001: 161-162). Actor preferences remain fixed as they negotiate agreements through signaling and arguing as well as more coercive bargaining. This is a very familiar approach to international regimes, which suggests that cooperation flourishes when actors conceive of their interests in terms of absolute, rather than relative, gains. Communication, in the limited sense of an exchange of information, stabilizes expectations about the future. Interests, or preferences, remain private knowledge.

Communicative action, in the deeper sense, seeks understanding through the development of common knowledge. Argumentation remains "rational," but debate can redefine the participants' goals and self-understandings. Three criteria set the stage for such moral deliberation: actors speak what they understand to be true; they invoke the rightness or validity of their normative claims; and, by respecting everyone's sincerity, they accept each other as equals. The definition of interests depends on membership in specific communities, and change occurs through persuasion. Presumably when the conditions necessary for communicative action prevail, norms of cooperation spread. Even in situations lacking all these ideal conditions, diplomacy remains a practice of communicating normative judgments that cannot be not fully captured by the notion of instrumental rationality. Rhetoric can have constitutive effects.

Although Adler does not adopt the language of communicative action theory, these characteristics resonate with his picture of arms control. Epistemic communities develop a common stock of knowledge that they understand to be based on scientific findings about the arms race. They invoke this knowledge as they seek to persuade other elites within governments of the validity of their claims that limiting the development of new weapons will stabilize the international system (and hence provide greater security to all). Informed by the common knowledge of scientists on both sides, policy-makers, who consider each other their equals, communicate directly in face-to-face treaty negotiations. New definitions of security, such as fear of nuclear devastation, transform interests (and perhaps identities). States then reach agreements, including previously unthinkable arms control policies.

Since states and their representatives negotiate all the time, communicative action theory can apply to all kinds of issues within both bilateral and multilateral settings, providing general conclusions about the conditions which lead to successful negotiations or normatively desirable outcomes. As Risse and Sikkink (1999) demonstrate in their assessment of human rights activism, communicative action theory highlights processes of constitutive interaction, such as socialization. And these can be distinguished from instrumental ones, such as strategic adaptation. The point is not whether the ideal conditions of communicative action hold but to categorize and evaluate the dynamics in a relationship.

Yet the list of ideal conditions should not be dismissed, since they draw attention to the context of negotiations and, therefore, a formulation of the conditions under which communicative interactions would be more likely than instrumental actions (Müller 2004: 401-404; see also Schimmelfennig 2003). Who is entitled to communicate? Speakers in a debate or rational argument must share a "lifeworld." This amalgamation of common experience, history, culture, and modes of interpretation provides grounds for validity claims. State and non-state actors frame their appeals based on community membership, which they may define in sub-national, national, transnational, or even global terms.

Analysts should expect to see aspiring participants petition for a right to speak at multilateral negotiations in terms of a shared lifeworld. Researchers are more likely to find the preconditions for communicative action in negotiations among members of the European Union over defense, agriculture, currency, or enlargement than in East-West negotiations over the status of a reunited Germany or multilateral negotiations over human rights or the environment. Non-governmental participants can also appeal to an increasingly global lifeworld, as they did in negotiations leading to the creation of the International Criminal Court (Struett 2005). Indeed, the UN has institutionalized an expanded definition of the "international community" by recognizing non-state actors to participate in its deliberations. Not all actors will be accepted as negotiation partners but researchers may find plenty of evidence that those excluded from deliberations still invoke common histories and shared cultures in order to claim a right to speak, as did South Africa in response to international sanctions.

These debates over the existence of a lifeworld bear striking resemblance to older divides between those who characterize the international system as anarchical versus those who conceive of it as a society of states (Bull 1977; Dunne 1998). Echoing Habermas's belief that it is possible to achieve universal consensus on certain norms, Lose (2001) goes farther than the international society approach to suggest that a lifeworld can transcend state (or individual) interests in favor of a "general interest." Indeed, claims for the universality of certain human rights norms follow this line of thinking, although not without challenges from critics who see these as a manifestation of a particular form of liberal ideology (see Chapter 3).

We treat this as an empirical, rather than ontological, question. First, to distinguish members of a particular community, analysts would ask who embraces human rights norms. Identities, in this view, serve as precursors to interests. In negotiations, researchers then witness whether participants make appeals that clearly distinguish between common values, experiences, and norms, on the one hand, and instrumental calculations, on the other. For example, Risse (2000) points to a shift in the responses of dictatorships during meetings of the UN Human Rights Commission, from ridiculing human rights norms to debating the specific accusations against them, as evidence of successful communicative action. Although these dictators may accept the norms of the international community, analysts still need to assess whether communicative interaction actually leads to changes in their articulation of interests.

After determining who the relevant negotiating participants are, what they are negotiating about, and why, researchers can predict whether communicative action might indeed lead to the transformation of the speakers' interests or simply strategic shifts in policy positions. For example, to underscore the causal role of communicative interaction, Risse asserts that Gorbachev decided during a specific meeting of the Four Power negotiations that a reunited Germany could join NATO if it wanted to, much to the surprise and dismay of other members of the Soviet delegation to the talks. Similarly, Checkel (2005) carefully parses the language of discussions within the European Union to distinguish evidence of diverse mechanisms of socialization. Such micro-level process-tracing pays very close attention to content and sequencing in the language of negotiations, drawing as much as possible on interviews, position papers, memoranda, and records of proceedings, to disentangle the explanatory differences between communicative and strategic action. The main difference between this use of process-tracing and that used to examine decision-making is that the latter tends to search for evidence of participants' motivations that lead to particular policy outcomes, whereas communicative action theorists seek to delineate processes of interaction.

Several aspects of communicative action theory remain unresolved, despite its value as a tool to distinguish between instrumental and constitutive processes. Reliance on the lifeworld as a precondition gives rise to the criticism that the approach is ethnocentric. Perhaps because it applies more easily in Europe, the theory downplays power differentials that preclude participants in international settings addressing each other as equals. Many former colonies, for instance, remain secondary partners in deliberations about aid or the impact of interest rates on their currencies. Even analysts of Europe should not take for granted common histories or equal standing, as contestation over regional integration demonstrates. (This debate mirrors the one over inequality and ethics in Chapter 3.)

One response is to pay more attention to the power of language in these negotiations, to see whether communicative action theory can apply across socio-historical contexts and when actors have some capacity to define the normative boundaries of a lifeworld. As an alternative conceptualization of constitutive interaction through speech acts, the notion of language games shifts away from debate about rationality and back to the tensions between intentionality and subjectivity.

### Language Games

A second strand of speech act theory draws more on Wittgenstein, Austin, and/or Searle (see Suggested Readings) to explore how meanings make certain types of action possible or necessary. Onuf (1998) suggests that communication falls into one of three possible types: instructions, directives, and commissives. Some utterances, such as "I promise," are actions which embody norms and expectations. In other cases, such as "I will increase my weapons if you increase yours," language expresses a reaction to another actor's behavior (Kratochwil 1989). Promises and threats make sense because they are intersubjectively understood. By emphasizing the performative role of language, this version of speech act theory links norms and rules (terms that the theory generally treats as interchangeable) to interests and behavior.

These analysts look at speech in both closed-door negotiations and public pronouncements as moves embedded in particular "language games," where the actors involved in talking and listening are aware of the "grammars" that give meaning to their utterances (Fierke 1998, 2002). These grammars are contexts comprised of specific rules of the game that circumscribe the range of possible actions. These "rules" differ from "representations." The language game approach relies on metaphors, including the most fundamental one of a "game," as guides to action, rather than linguistic oppositions, such as the tropes that define Self and Other (see Chapter 4). For example, Fierke's (1998) analysis of Cold War discourse draws attention to recurring themes of *building* alliances, *restoring* US/Soviet military might, and *maintaining* stability through first and second-strike rationales. The metaphors underpinning interactions within an alliance or security community differ from those of a balance of power grammar, such as the "common European home" vocabulary that Gorbachev and others put forth at the end of the Cold War. The same utterance can convey a different meaning depending on the grammatical context.

Researchers discern grammars inductively, by reading widely in primary and secondary materials, such as mainstream and critical analyses of the Cold War, official and non-governmental documents, negotiation proceedings, press statements, and interviews. Unlike historical narrative, which also uses metaphors of action gleaned from many of these same sources to present a causal storyline (see Chapter 3), speech act theory concentrates on interactions. This form of interpretation, like all others, will inevitably be influenced by the researcher's own commitments. But speech act theory does provide a less ethnocentric context of meaning than the notion of a lifeworld, because its notion of grammars and rules does not require participants to share deep-rooted histories. It also avoids the reification that can limit the usefulness of culture and civilization as analytical categories, as in Wendt's (1999) characterization of Hobbesian, Lockean, and Kantian logics, because games are multidimensional and overlapping.

Actors know what to expect from each others' actions when rules are relatively stable and widely shared. For example, governments tend to *restore* or *maintain* military might. Many moves are possible. Fierke (1998) sees critics of superpower foreign policies engaged in *dismantling moves* during Cold War security debates. And, translating Thomas's (2001) work on social movement mobilization into speech act vocabulary, regime opponents might also be capable of *building moves*: West European peace activists and their East European human rights counterparts incorporated each others' goals into a transnational articulation of joint interests in disarmament and respect for political rights. However, the notion of framing, which Thomas applies in his analysis, grants more *causal* effect to social movements than does Fierke's contextual analysis, which focuses our attention on norms as *conditions* for their activism. But fundamentally, both scholars point in the same direction: some moves change the rules of the game (what we label "system change" in Chapter 2).

To understand the transition from one dominant grammar to another, Fierke suggests a two stage process. Merely proposing alternative rules, what she calls "immanent critique," denaturalizes the rules of the game. Dialogue then determines whether these alternatives become the new rules. If (or when) these alternatives become the regular way of doing things, and discourses about interests incorporate them into part of normal practice, analysts recognize them as new rules. For example, one key element in the disintegration of the Cold War was the Four Power agreement on a reunited Germany, which stipulated that Germany would be a member of NATO unless it decided otherwise. This agreement challenged the conventional wisdom that it was in the Soviet Union's interest to keep Germany officially neutral and out of any alliance system.

Since the rules of the game create roles for "players," changes in the rules of the game also alter their identities and interests. This mutually constitutive transformation is manifest in major alterations in discourse, including appeals to the rules of the game. Superpower arms treaties, such as the Intermediate Nuclear Force agreement of

1987, provided for the actual disarming of nuclear weapons, rather than merely caps on future accumulation. Reaching these accords undermined the conventional wisdom that it was in US interests not to agree to any arms reductions due to the Soviets' advantage in megatonnage as well as their alleged untrustworthiness. In the subsequent two decades, such agreements have become standard procedure. The Soviets, in turn, relaxed their long-standing belief in the need for a "cordon sanitaire" to control Warsaw Pact countries. Thus the epistemic communities of Adler's arms control analysis become players in a larger process of rewriting the fundamental rules of the game, and assessments of their activities expand beyond the range of policy outcomes to incorporate rules of interaction (and thus process).

Of course, new rules do not eliminate contestation or automatically stabilize interests, nor do they limit the number of games played in future interactions. Fierke stresses the significance of simultaneity and overlaps during the Cold War. The unraveling of a grammar can generate more than one new game, each with its own rules: specific negotiations, such as those within the institutions governing the world economy; the creation of new organizations, such as the League of Nations and United Nations; and major transformations, such the beginning and ending of the Cold War. Grammars and games can appear at many levels of analysis.

As the number of possible games and instability in the rules increase, it becomes difficult to delimit feasible research projects. Despite being able to offer insights into mechanisms of change at the macro-level of the international system, speech act theory may be best suited for analysis of international regimes, where researchers make assumptions about the boundaries of relevant issue-specific discourses. In such a setting, the complementarities between linguistic and rationalist approaches to games become more apparent (Fierke and Nicholson 2001; see also O'Neill 1999).

## Implications

All of these studies call into question the equation of interests with the pursuit of material resources. For constructivists, interests are the product of constitutive processes that lead people, as individuals and members of collectivities, to synthesize a wide range of needs and desires. Even the dramatic military realignment that marked the end of the Cold War came about through the communicative and instrumental actions of state and non-state actors on multiple levels, not simply as the result of bargains between two superpowers. The myriad relationships and interactions that comprise the international system overlap, making it impossible to characterize one single, overarching distribution of (military) power.

People may pursue power, but power defined in social as well as material terms. States still write most of the rules of the game(s), which reaffirm them as the primary actors on the world stage. And since most speech reinforces these rules, power becomes vested in these grammars. Yet other actors do sometimes attempt to destabilize those rules, perhaps through persuasive argumentation, as communicative action theory proposes, or through disruptive protest, as social movement theories would predict. Non-state actors can exercise influence over how people conceive of their place in the environment or how elites view the ethical implications of nuclear devastation. Some of them may also successfully negotiate for a voice in policy debates by invoking some rules of the game (agenda-setting), as a way to gain access to arenas where their proposal for alternative rules may get adopted. From there, analysts can tease out the disparate power relationships that language games create between governments, social movements, international organizations, and other actors, to see how different "communities" of people articulate, promote, and debate their interests.

We hope that researchers wrestle further with the emphasis we have given to processes over outcomes, instead of relying on the overdrawn one between norms and interests. Yet our skepticism about a narrow definition of instrumental behavior based as the pursuit of material gain does not resolve debates over intentionality and rationality. We call on constructivists to explore further the cognitive and communicative dimensions of rationality. That research agenda requires deeper dialogue between constructivists and other IR theorists. As we note in our concluding reflections, professional as well as philosophical barriers circumscribe such debates.

# Chapter Six

# Conclusions

We hope that by juxtaposing a wide variety of research designs we have made inroads against rigid distinctions between "mainstream" versus "radical" constructivism. Significant similarities emerge, notably the use of discursive evidence and socio-historical context to capture a broad notion of power. All of these studies start with basic assumptions grounded in an ontology of mutual constitution, make logical claims based on some indicators (or measures) of what people perceive to be the world in which they live, and assess alternative arguments. The best work remains self-aware of the ways in which the experiences and assumptions of researchers influence all stages of this scholarly process.

By exposing researchers to a wide variety of (perhaps unfamiliar) methods in the preceding chapters, we suggest ways to refine strategies for describing, analyzing, and evaluating the relationships between structure and agency. Because we avoid the imposition of a narrow or dogmatic view of social science, no simple methodological synthesis emerges, nor should we expect one. Philosophical debates between positivists and post-positivists will remain unresolved for valid reasons, including the indeterminacy of evidence in the social sciences (Hookway and Pettit, eds. 1978; Little 1991; Rosenau 1992; Green and Shapiro 1994). Since constructivists still have much more work to do in sorting out the dynamics of constitutive processes, we believe that a *grounded* dialogue along this epistemological spectrum remains a valuable endeavor. Ultimately, our aim in writing this volume is to improve understanding about world politics, not to defend pluralism for its own sake.

But Hellmann (2003a: 123) rightly asks, in a recent forum on dialogue and synthesis in IR, "If dialogue is so highly appreciated, why is there so much monologue?" Our basic response is that scholars need to learn the vocabulary used by those in other "camps" in order to appreciate the insights of alternative approaches. Each of the preceding chapters attempts this type of translation, and we hope that others will elaborate in their subsequent research. Yet merely being better listeners of monologues that have been translated into familiar language does not produce true dialogue. That requires intellectual openness, which we must count on our readers to supply.

We assume that anyone who has read this far does indeed seek dialogue. Therefore, we reflect in this final chapter on a few aspects of the research and publication processes that reinforce barriers to greater discussion across the epistemological divide. And in keeping with the overall constructivist claim that structure and agency constitute each other, we suggest a few strategic adaptations and potential reforms that might reduce those barriers. First, we return to the question of standards for evaluating scholarship that we raised in the first chapter. We then comment briefly on professional dynamics, which has been an undercurrent throughout all of the chapters.

## The Question of Standards

Because constructivist ontology rejects the notion of an objective reality against which analysts test the accuracy of interpretations, "falsifiability" cannot be the goal. Researchers can do no more than contrast interpretations against other interpretations. Not all interpretations are equally valid. Based upon an inductive survey of the standards invoked by constructivist researchers—not from the deductive imposition of an epistemological orthodoxy—we made a case in Chapter 1 for the incorporation of the widest range of available evidence in pursuit of coherent descriptions and explanations. This standard reinforces Harvey and Cobb's conclusion that, "Although logic will not necessarily enhance our capacity to find the 'truth,' it does force all of us to refine, clarify, and defend what we believe to be true" (2003: 147). Such debate over alternative interpretations is the basis for scholarly dialogue.

We do not claim that constructivists have no problems in establishing the validity of truth claims. Indeed, that is why we presented a range of research tools, as well as commentary on trade-offs between them. Any choice of method necessarily draws on select evidence and limits the range of possible interpretations. In defending these interpretations, scholars will inevitably weigh generality against detail, even though neither will make universal claims. And since there is always a give-and-take process between data collection and refinement of the research design, researchers must remain open to unexpected evidence that appears to challenge central arguments or hypotheses.

Yet even these flexible and inclusive guidelines mask assumptions about logic and interpretation. We cannot completely sideline meta-theoretical considerations, because analysts inevitably formulate questions and select methodologies based on (implicit or explicit) understandings of social science and the proper role of the researcher. Theories tell researchers what counts as "relevant" evidence. For instance, the selection of linguistic and non-linguistic texts depends, in part, on alternative notions of subjectivity, intentionality, or rationality. In addition, as Waever (1998: 694) points out in his comparison of European and US academic practices, different scholarly traditions privilege certain styles of presentation which become the standard of a "coherent" argument.

Participant-observation (Chapter 2) and ethnography (Chapter 3) best capture the *inter*subjective nature of reality and dialogical aspects of knowledge claims. These methods openly implicate the researcher in a way that turns to their advantage what tends to be derided by others as bias. Because these techniques involve intensive interaction, the analyst and the subject of analysis may influence each other. By creating experiential knowledge, these methods force the researcher to confront interpretive problems on a different level than that of an interviewer who only briefly encounters an interviewee. This requires more openness to hermeneutic issues, as well as a different style of communicating research findings, often in forms more akin to autobiography than history.

Yet their inherently contemporaneous nature also limits the range of applicability in historical settings, precluding any claims that these represent the "best" tools for all constructivist research.

One might conclude, in turn, that methods at the other end of the epistemological spectrum, specifically those that employ quantitative measures, are antithetical to constructivism. Yet statistical studies have been effective in demonstrating wide-ranging diffusion of practices on a scale that specific cases would be unable to do (e.g., Meyer 1979; Finnemore 1993; some contributors to Katzenstein, ed. 1996; Boli and Thomas, eds. 1999). As long as we keep in mind that quantitative evidence, distinguished by its reliance on a larger number of cases (or "observations"), has no higher claim to accuracy or objectivity, constructivists should not limit their tools of analysis. (More sophisticated statistical techniques, furthermore, are not limited to the simple regressions that are often all that get taught in elementary methods courses.) Researchers can effectively use statistical evidence to describe and analyze properties of, or patterns in, language, as long as interpretations of these numbers remain sensitive to socio-historical context. The same can be said for models based on rationality or any other assumption; they are heuristics for crafting logical arguments that carry no special validity compared to other forms of theorizing (e.g., Hoffmann 2005). Indeed, because any type of comparison or assessment starts with a baseline expectation, it holds interpretive, and hence ethical, implications. This should be acknowledged when using qualitative as well as quantitative tools. We encourage *creative* use of all methods, as long as researchers do not claim objectivity or universal truth.

## The Nature of the Profession

Combining methods to explore compelling issues from a variety of standpoints can lead to fruitful insights—but it is not always easy to get such work published. For example, major journals, notably *International Organization*, have perpetuated the notion that constructivism is one of three paradigms, with clear boundaries that distinguish it from Realism and Liberalism, and silence Marxism. This framing of the scholarly debate holds implications for professional status and job security, illustrating how micro-level practices reinforce institutionalized power disparities. Scholarly survival ("publish or perish") reinforces rewards for writing in the language of rival paradigms, as people self-identify with particular paradigms and have labels imposed upon their work. Hellmann points out that one of the barriers to dialogue is high "personal stakes" that lead to a professional context in which "we benefit more from arguing against each other than from learning with each other" (2003b: 147). Kratochwil formulates this position in more psychological terms when he claims that, "The desire to win, to stand one's ground, perhaps not surprisingly, is most of the time stronger than the genuine search for an acceptable solution to a problem" (2003: 125). Paradigmatic camps, in other words, might provide researchers with a sense of scholarly security. This professional dynamic is not restricted to the "American" side of the IR discipline, although we wrote this book from within that context.

As Kratochwil notes, the answer is not simply the creation of a "flood of publications whose function is to provide an outlet for various citation cartels" (2003: 128). Fostering dialogue requires being attuned to issues of audience, or what Neumann calls "addressivity": who is being addressed and in what manner (2003: 138). Those seeking to publish in, and influence the trajectory of, the US-dominated IR field need to recognize the increasing attention being paid to qualitative methods as part of a broader debate about epistemology in Political Science (Monroe, ed. 2005; Yanow and Schwartz-Shea, eds. 2006). Those working in environments less constrained by the disciplining effects of Political Science on IR scholarship more readily find voice in European outlets. There is no need to overturn behavioralist or rationalist orthodoxies where general acceptance of historical and sociological assumptions prevails (Waever 1998).

We believe that the strategic use of alternative citations can counter dominant theories. Yet we remain wary of identifying scholarly cartels based on geography (Klotz 2001). Presumably "radical" or "critical" approaches flourish in Europe but not in the United States, where "conventional" or "mainstream" constructivism reigns. Elaborating upon Price and Reus-Smit's (1998) call (coming from the Canadian and Australian margins) for "liaison" between critical theory and constructivism, we probed the methodological stakes of this putative divide, rather than letting these concerns be side-lined as merely another manifestation of US-based academics' obsession with social science. Similarly, both Milliken (2001) and Fierke (2001) have suggested criteria for assessing "better" discourse analyses in ways that bridge "modern" and "postmodern" conceptualizations of language. With degrees from US universities and jobs in Europe, they also defy easy classification based on geography.

Researchers inevitably have social identities of their own, and we do not claim to remove scholarship from its temporal and spatial context. In keeping with the admonitions in Chapter 4 to remain sensitive to fluidity and multiplicity, we caution again fixing scholarly identities too rigidly in the characterization of a constructivist divide. These play out in incredibly diverse ways in empirical work.

## Prospects for Building Bridges within Constructivism

Constructivists cannot avoid the ethical dimension of our work—norms, rules, representations, culture, ideology, and all the other forms of intersubjective understandings that are at the core of the constructivist ontology cannot be analyzed in a value-free context (Price and Reus-Smit 1998; Lynch 1999a and 2006). The definition of the term terrorism, for instance, can connote a range of normative positions but most often, at least in IR scholarship, it refers to the use of violence to incite fear. That definition signifies an illegitimate activity and devalues any particular goals actors seek to achieve through such means. If analysts take that definition for granted, they are unlikely to probe how or why government officials, public commentators, and academics construct this particular meaning. Nor are they likely to take seriously the grievances and aspirations of those who resort to unsanctioned violence. Once analysts delimit the range of questions, certain moral positions become embedded in particular research agendas and the policy prescriptions that result.

We call on our readers to be attuned to the ways in which research reinforces or counters the inherent inequalities that dominant discourses create. Yet we caution against translating ethical assumptions into particular tools of analysis. No method should be granted the moral high ground. A researcher might want to examine whether and why "terrorism" (following the mainstream definition) has increased since the end of the Cold War. Causal process-tracing can address this question from an agency-oriented perspective by exploring US foreign policy decisions from the Cold War period to the present. This same researcher might then use genealogy to query the definition of terrorism and how the use of the term evolves over time. Furthermore, an analysis of government narratives of terrorist activity contrasted against the narratives of those labeled terrorists could bridge agency-oriented and structural views. Finally, the researcher could supplement all of these other approaches with a frame analysis to grasp how elites delegitimize the actions of those labeled terrorists and how violent social groups challenge state behavior. These are examples of complementarities among analytical tools, not a formula for doing empirical research on terrorism or any other issue. Throughout this book, we have offered focused questions to guide the selection of suitable methods for a range of research questions.

Perhaps it is ironic that constructivists have been divided primarily at the level of meta-theory, since our rejection of universal knowledge claims and our emphasis on contextualized interpretations are inherently well-suited to problem-oriented research. If more "critical" constructivists admit to making generalizations while more "conventional" constructivists concede difficulties in treating fluid meanings as variables, then we can move forward in our efforts to understand the nature of and limits to social change.

# Appendix

# Suggested Readings

Debates among constructivists within IR draw upon and mirror trends across the social sciences and humanities. These cross-disciplinary debates, often referred to as the "linguistic" or "cultural" turn in social theory, are rooted in twentieth century debates about language. Social scientists have been arguing ever since Max Weber's *Methodology of the Social Sciences* (1949; the original essays were published between 1904 and 1917) and *Sociology of Religion* (1963; first published in 1922). Some classic works that remain generally useful today include Fred Dallmayr and Thomas McCarthy's *Understanding and Social Inquiry* (1977), Richard Bernstein's *The Restructuring of Social and Political Theory* (1976), and Peter Berger and Thomas Luckmann's *The Social Construction of Reality* (1966). David Hiley, James Bohman, and Richard Shusterman's *The Interpretive Turn* (1991) and Ian Hacking's *The Social Construction of What?* (1999) provide more recent takes. *The Return of Grand Theory in the Human Sciences*, edited by Quentin Skinner (1985), covers many of the main interlocutors in philosophy, while *Interpretive Social Sciences: A Reader*, edited by Paul Rabinow and William Sullivan (1979), supplies views from those pursuing empirical research in a range of disciplines.

The linguistic turn took hold across the social sciences in the 1940s and 1950s. In this view, language does not represent objective facts. Rather, both fact and language reflect intersubjective understandings. Classics include Ludwig Wittgenstein's *Philosophical Investigation* (1958) and Peter Winch's *The Idea of a Social Science and Its Relation to Philosophy* (1958). Along with J. L. Austin's (1962) and John Searle's (1969) work on speech-act theory, their legacies are manifest in modern and post-modern variants of social construction. Strong evidence of their legacies come from Anthony Giddens's notion of "structuration," which he develops in *Central Problems of Social Theory* (1979) and *The Constitution of Society* (1984), as well as Jürgen Habermas's *Theory of Communicative Action* (1984, 1987) and Pierre Bourdieu's *Language and Symbolic Power* (1991).

Those influenced more by the "cultural turn" usually appeal to Michel Foucault. His *Discipline and Punish* (1977) and *History of Sexuality* (1978, 1985) draw attention to the relationship between knowledge, power, and social reality. *Michel Foucault, Beyond Structuralism and Hermeneutics*, by Hubert Dreyfus and Paul Rabinow (1982) is a classic exposition of the implications of his work for social science. For Foucault's own explanation of his method and the macro-historical concerns which animate it, see *The Foucault Effect: Studies in Governmentality*, edited by Graham Burchell, Colin Gordon, and Peter Miller (1991). Other strong influences include Friedrich Nietzsche's *On the Genealogy of Morality* (1994), Louis Althusser (1971) on the relationship between ideology and state power, and Antonio Gramsci's exploration of culture and hegemony in *Prison Notebooks* (1971).

These debates have entered the IR lexicon through various disciplinary avenues. Constructivists are often drawn explicitly or implicitly into controversies among historians. A classic exposition of the interpretive problems is E. H. Carr's *What Is History?* (1961). William Sewell's retrospective, "Whatever Happened to the 'Social' in Social History?" (2001), concentrates specifically on the shift from social to cultural history and makes a case for a more synthetic approach that breaks down the distinction between quantitative and interpretive work (among other points). *From Reliable Sources*, by Martha Howell and Walter Prevenier (2001), situates these debates in the evolution of historiography, as well as providing a helpful discussion of some of the nuts and bolts of dealing with archival and other types of evidence. Eckhardt Fuchs and Bendikt Stuchtey call into question the Eurocentric focus of most of these debates in *Across Cultural Borders* (2002).

Drawing on literary criticism, Hayden White's *The Content of the Form: Narrative Discourse and Historical Representation* (1987) reevaluates the concept of narrative in historiography. Other useful sources on narrative include Donald Polkinghorne, *Narrative Knowing and the Human Sciences* (1988); Potter Abbott, *The Cambridge Introduction to Narrative* (2002); and the range of works by Paul Ricoeur, including *Time and Narrative, Vol. 1* (1984). For Ricoeur's thought applied to the social sciences, see his *Hermeneutics and the Human Sciences: Essays on Language, Action, and Interpretation* (1981). The original hermeneutical enterprise concerned biblical studies; in addition to Ricoeur, see André LaCocque and David Pellaur, *Thinking Biblically: Exegetical and Hermeneutical Studies* (1998). Stuart Hall (1985) and Gayatri Spivak (1987) have been particularly effective at adding non-European perspectives to these debates. Their work in cultural studies easily elides into debates in anthropology over methods, particularly the inherent relationship in ethnography between participant-observation and power. In addition to Clifford Geertz's classic compilation of essays, *The Interpretation of Cultures* (1973), see James Clifford and George Marcus, eds., *Writing Culture: The Poetics and Politics of Ethnography* (1986).

No short list of recommended books and articles could possibly do justice to the philosophical issues underlying these debates. Nor do we suggest that this volume can—or should—put an end to discussions of ontology, epistemology, methodology, or validity. We encourage our readers to deepen their explorations of these interdisciplinary writings as they develop their own research agendas.

# References

Abbott, Porter (2002). *The Cambridge Introduction to Narrative*. New York: Cambridge University Press.

Abdelal, Rawi (2001). *National Purpose in the World Economy: Post-Soviet States in Comparative Perspective*. Ithaca, NY: Cornell University Press.

Ackerly, Brooke A. (2000). *Political Theory and Feminist Social Criticism*. New York: Cambridge University Press.

Ackerly, Brooke A., and Jacqui True (2001). "Transnational Justice: The Contribution of Feminism to Critical International Relations Theory." Unpublished paper, University of Southern California (April).

Adcock, Robert and David Collier (2001). "Measurement Validity: A Shared Standard for Qualitative and Quantitative Research," *American Political Science Review* 95 (3): 529–546.

Adler, Emanuel (1992). "The Emergence of Cooperation: National Epistemic Communities and the International Evolution of the Idea of Nuclear Arms Control," *International Organization* 46 (1): 101–145.

Adler, Emanuel (1997). "Seizing the Middle Ground: Constructivism in World Politics," *European Journal of International Relations* 3 (3): 319–363.

Adler, Emanuel (2002). "Constructivism and International Relations," in *Handbook of International Relations*, ed. Walter Carlsnaes, Thomas Risse, and Beth Simmons. Newbury Park, CA: Sage.

Adler, Emanuel and Steven Bernstein (2005). "Knowledge in Power: The Epistemic Construction of Global Governance," in *Power in Global Governance*, ed. Michael Barnett and Raymond Duvall. New York: Cambridge University Press.

Althusser, Louis (1971). "Ideology and the Ideological State Apparatuses (Notes Toward an Investigation)," in *Lenin and Philosophy and Other Essays*, trans. B. Brewster. London: New Left Books.

Appadurai, Arjun (1996). *Modernity at Large: Cultural Dimensions of Globalization*. Minneapolis: University of Minnesota Press

Ashley, Richard K. (1984). "The Poverty of Neorealism." *International Organization* 38 (2): 225–286.

Austin, J. L. (1962). *How to Do Things With Words*. Cambridge, MA: Harvard University Press.

Ba, Alice and Matthew Hoffmann (2003). "Making and Remaking the World for IR 101: A Resource for Teaching Social Constructivism in Introductory Classes," *International Studies Perspectives* 4 (1): 15–33.

Barkin, J. Samuel (2003). "Realist Constructivism," *International Studies Review* 5 (3): 325–342.

Barkin, J. Samuel and Bruce Cronin (1994). "The State and the Nation: Changing Norms and the Rules of Sovereignty in International Relations," *International Organization* 48 (1): 107–130.

Barnett, Michael (1993). "Peacekeeping, Indifference, and Genocide in Rwanda," in *Cultures of Insecurity: States, Communities, and the Production of Danger*, ed. Jutta Weldes, Mark Laffey, Hugh Gusterson, and Raymond Duvall. Minneapolis: University of Minnesota Press.

Barnett, Michael (1998). *Dialogues in Arab Politics: Negotiations in Regional Order*. New York: Columbia University Press.

Barnett, Michael (2002). *Eyewitness to a Genocide: The United Nations and Rwanda*. Ithaca, NY: Cornell University Press.

Barnett, Michael and Martha Finnemore (1999). "The Politics, Power and Pathologies of International Organization," *International Organization* 53 (4): 699–732.

Barnett, Michael and Martha Finnemore (2004). *Rules for the World: International Organizations in Global Politics*. Ithaca, NY: Cornell University Press.

Beissinger, Mark (2002). *Nationalist Mobilization and the Collapse of the Soviet State*. New York: Cambridge University Press.

Berger, Peter L. and Thomas Luckmann (1966). *The Social Construction of Reality*. Garden City, NY: Doubleday.

Berman, Nathaniel (2000). "Modernism, Nationalism, and the Rhetoric of Reconstruction," in *Law and Moral Action in World Politics*, ed. Cecelia Lynch and Michael Loriaux. Minneapolis: University of Minnesota Press.

Bernstein, Richard J. (1976). *The Restructuring of Social and Political Theory*. New York: Harcourt, Brace and Jovanovich.

Biersteker, Thomas J. and Cynthia Weber, eds. (1996). *State Sovereignty as Social Construct*. Cambridge, UK: Cambridge University Press.

Black, David R. (1999). "'Not Cricket': The Effects and Effectiveness of the Sport Boycott," in *How Sanctions Work: Lessons from South Africa*, ed. Neta C. Crawford and Audie Klotz. Basingstoke, UK: Macmillan.

Blee, Kathleen and Verta Taylor (2002). "Semi-Structured Interviewing in Social Movement Research," in *Methods of Social Movement Research*, ed. Bert Klandermans and Suzanne Staggenborg. Mineapolis: University of Minnesota Press.

Boli, John and George M. Thomas, eds. (1999). *Constructing Global Culture: International Nongovernmental Organizations since 1875*. Stanford, CA: Stanford University Press.

Bosia, Michael J. (2005). "'Assassin!' AIDS and Neoliberal Reform in France," *New Political Science* 27 (3): 291–308.

Bourdieu, Pierre (1991). *Language and Symbolic Power.* Cambridge, MA: Harvard University Press.

Brubaker, Rogers and Frederick Cooper (2000). "Beyond Identity," *Theory and Society* 29 (1): 1–47.

Brysk, Alison (1993). "From Above and Below: Social Movements, the International System, and Human Rights in Argentina," *Comparative Political Studies* 26 (3): 259–285.

Brysk, Alison (2000). *From Tribal Village to Global Village: Indian Rights and International Relations in Latin America.* Stanford, CA: Stanford University Press.

Bukovansky, Mlada (1997). "American Identity and Neutral Rights from Independence to the War of 1812," *International Organization* 51 (2): 209–243.

Bull, Hedley (1977). *The Anarchical Society.* New York: Columbia University Press.

Burchell, Graham, Colin Gordon, and Peter Miller, eds. (1991). *The Foucault Effect: Studies in Governmentality.* Chicago: University of Chicago Press.

Campbell, David (1998a). *Writing Security: United States Foreign Policy and the Politics of Identity,* revised edition. Minneapolis: University of Minnesota Press.

Campbell, David (1998b). *National Deconstruction: Violence, Identity and Justice in Bosnia.* Minneapolis: University of Minnesota Press.

Carr, E. H. (1961). *What Is History?* New York: Knopf.

Cederman, Lars-Erik (1997). *Emergent Actors in World Politics: How States and Nations Develop and Dissolve.* Princeton, NJ: Princeton University Press.

Cederman, Lars-Erik and Christopher Daase (2003). "Endogenizing Corporate Identities: The Next Step in Constructivist IR Theory," *European Journal of International Relations* 9 (1): 5–35.

Checkel, Jeffrey T. (1997). "International Norms and Domestic Politics: Bridging the Rationalist – Constructivist Divide," *European Journal of International Relations* 3 (4): 473–495.

Checkel, Jeffrey T. (1999). "Norms, Institutions, and National Identity in Contemporary Europe," *International Studies Quarterly* 43 (1): 83–114.

Checkel, Jeffrey T. (2005). "International Institutions and Socialization in Europe: Introduction and Framework," *International Organization* 59 (4): 801–826.

Clemens, Elisabeth and Martin Hughes (2002). "Recovering Past Protest: Historical Research on Social Movements," in *Methods of Social Movement Research,* ed. Bert Klandermans and Suzanne Staggenborg. Minneapolis: University of Minnesota Press.

Clifford, James, and George Marcus, eds. (1986). *Writing Culture: The Poetics and Politics of Ethnography*. Berkeley: University of California Press.

Cohen, Jean L. and Andrew Arato (1992). *Civil Society and Political Theory*. Cambridge, MA: MIT Press.

Cohn, Carol (1987). "Sex and Death in the Rational World of Defense Intellectuals," *Signs* 12 (4): 687–718.

Cox, Robert W. (1986). "Social Forces, States, and World Orders: Beyond International Relations Theory," in *Neorealism and Its Critics*, ed. Robert O. Keohane. New York: Columbia University Press.

Cox, Robert W. (1989). "Production, the State, and Change in World Order," in *Global Changes and Theoretical Challenges*, ed. Ernst-Otto Czempiel and James N. Rosenau. New York: Macmillan.

Cox, Robert W. (1996). *Approaches to World Order.* Cambridge: Cambridge University Press.

Dallmayr, Fred and Thomas McCarthy, eds. (1977). *Understanding and Social Inquiry*. Notre Dame, IN: University of Notre Dame.

Der Derian, James (1987). *On Diplomacy: A Genealogy of Western Estrangement.* Oxford: Blackwell.

Di Alto, Stephanie (2004). "K i Ka Pono (Stand Up For Justice): Native Hawaiian-U.S. Relations, 1993–2003." Unpublished Ph.D. dissertation, University of California, Irvine.

Doty, Roxanne Lynn (1996). *Imperial Encounters: The Politics of Representation in North-South Relations*. Minneapolis: University of Minnesota Press.

Dreyfus, Hubert and Paul Rabinow (1982). *Michel Foucault, Beyond Structuralism and Hermeneutics*. Chicago: University of Chicago Press.

Dunn, Kevin (2003). *Imagining the Congo: The International Relations of Identity*. New York: Palgrave Macmillan.

Dunne, Timothy (1998). *Inventing International Society: A History of the English School.* Basingstoke: Macmillan.

Eickelman, Dale F. (1997). "Trans-state Islam and Security," in *Transnational Religion and Fading States*, ed. Susanne Hoeber Rudolph and James Piscatori. Boulder, CO: Westview.

Enloe, Cynthia (1990). *Bananas, Beaches, and Bases: Making Feminist Sense of International Politics*. Berkeley: University of California Press.

Enloe, Cynthia (1993). *The Morning After: Sexual Politics at the End of the Cold War.* Berkeley: University of California Press.

Fearon, James (1991). "Counterfactuals and Hypothesis Testing in Political Science," *World Politics* 43 (2): 169–195.

Fierke, K. M. (1998). *Changing Games, Changing Strategies: Critical Investigations in Security*. Manchester, UK: Manchester University Press.

Fierke, K. M. (2001). "Critical Methodology and Constructivism," in *Constructing International Relations: The Next Generation*, ed. Karin Fierke and Knud Erik Jørgensen. Armonk, NY: M. E. Sharpe.

Fierke, K. M. (2002). "Links Across the Abyss: Language and Logic in International Relations," *International Studies Quarterly* 46 (3): 331–354.

Fierke, K. M. and Michael Nicholson (2001). "Divided by a Common Language: Formal and Constructivist Approaches to Games," *Global Society* 15 (1): 7–25.

Finnemore, Martha (1993). "Norms, Culture and World Politics: Insights from Sociology's Institutionalism," *International Organization* 50 (2): 325–347.

Finnemore, Martha (1996). *National Interests in International Society*. Ithaca, NY: Cornell University Press.

Finnemore, Martha (2003). *The Purpose of Intervention: Changing Beliefs about the Use of Force*. Ithaca, NY: Cornell University Press.

Forum (2004). "Bridging the Gap: Toward a Realist-Constructivist Dialogue," *International Studies Review* 6 (2): 337–352.

Forum (2006). "Moving Beyond the Agent-Structure Debate," *International Studies Review*, 8 (2): 355–381.

Foucault, Michel (1977). *Discipline and Punish: The Birth of the Prison*. New York: Vintage.

Foucault, Michel (1978). *The History of Sexuality, Volume 1: An Introduction*. New York: Vintage.

Foucault, Michel (1985). *The History of Sexuality, Volume 2: The Use of Pleasure*. New York: Vintage.

Fraser, Nancy (1989). *Unruly Practices: Power, Discourse and Gender in Contemporary Social Theory*. Minneapolis: University of Minnesota Press.

Fuchs, Eckhardt and Bendikt Stuchtey, eds. (2002). *Across Cultural Borders: Historiography in Global Perspective*. Lanham, MD: Rowman and Littlefield.

Gamson, William A. (1992). "The Social Psychology of Collective Action," in *Frontiers in Social Movement Theory*, ed. Aldon D. Morris and Carol McClurg Mueller. New Haven: Yale University Press.

Geertz, Clifford (1973). *The Interpretation of Cultures: Selected Essays*. New York: Basic Books.

Geertz, Clifford (1979). "From the Native's Point of View: On the Nature of Anthropological Understanding," in *Interpretive Social Science: A Reader*, ed. Paul Rabinow and William Sullivan. Berkeley: University of California Press.

Geertz, Clifford (1983). *Local Knowledge: Further Essays in Interpretive Anthropology*. New York: Basic Books.

George, Alexander L. and Andrew Bennett (2005). *Case Studies and Theory Development in the Social Sciences*. Cambridge, MA: MIT Press.

George, Alexander L and Timothy J. McKeown (1985). "Case Studies and Theories of Organizational Decision-Making," *Advances in Information Processing in Organizations* 2: 21–58.

Giddens, Anthony (1979). *Central Problems in Social Theory.* Berkeley: University of California Press.

Giddens, Anthony (1984). *The Constitution of Society: Outline of the Theory of Structuration.* Berkeley: University of California Press.

Goff, Patricia and Kevin Dunn (2004a). "Introduction," in *Identity and Global Politics: Empirical and Theoretical Elaborations,* ed. Patricia Goff and Kevin Dunn. New York: Palgrave Macmillan.

Goff, Patricia and Kevin Dunn (2004b). *Identity and Global Politics: Empirical and Theoretical Elaborations.* New York: Palgrave Macmillan.

Goffman, Erving (1974). *Frame Analysis.* New York: Harper.

Goldstein, Joshua (2001). *War and Gender: How Gender Shapes the War System and Vice Versa.* New York: Cambridge University Press.

Gramsci, Antonio (1971). *Selections from the Prison Notebooks.* New York: International Publishers.

Green, Donald and Ian Shapiro (1994). *Pathologies of Rational Choice.* New Haven, CT: Yale University Press.

Grovogui, Siba N. (1996). *Sovereigns, Quasi Sovereigns, and Africans: Race and Self-Determination in International Law.* Minneapolis: University of Minnesota Press.

Grovogui, Siba N. (2006). *Beyond Eurocentrism and Anarchy: Memories of International Order and Institutions.* New York: Palgrave Macmillan.

Gupta, Akhil and James Ferguson, eds. (1997). *Anthropological Locations: Boundaries and Grounds of a Field Science.* Berkeley: University of California Press.

Gusterson, Hugh (1996). *Nuclear Rites: A Weapons Laboratory at the End of the Cold War.* Berkeley: University of California Press.

Guzzini, Stefano (2000). "A Reconstruction of Constructivism in International Relations," *European Journal of International Relations* 6 (2): 147–182.

Haas, Peter M., ed. (1992). "Knowledge, Power and International Policy Coordination," special issue of *International Organization* 46 (1).

Habermas, Jürgen (1984). *Theory of Communicative Action, Vol. I: Reason and The Rationalization of Society,* trans. Thomas McCarthy. Boston: Beacon Press.

Habermas, Jürgen (1987). *Theory of Communicative Action, Vol. II: Lifeworld and System: A Critique of Functionalist Reason,* trans. Thomas McCarthy. Boston: Beacon Press.

Hacking, Ian (1999). *The Social Construction of What?* Cambridge, MA: Harvard University Press.

Hall, Rodney Bruce (1997). "Moral Authority as a Power Resource," *International Organization* 51 (4): 591–622.

Hall, Stuart (1985). "Signification, Representation, Ideology: Althusser and the Post-Structuralist Debates," *Critical Studies in Mass Communication* 2 (2): 91–114.

Halttunen, Karen (1999). "Cultural History and the Challenge of Narrativity," in *Beyond the Cultural Turn*, ed. Victoria E. Bonnell and Lynn Hunt. Berkeley: University of California Press.

Harvey Frank and Joel Cobb (2003). "Multiple Dialogues Layered Syntheses, and the Limits of Expansive Cumulation," *International Studies Review* 5(1): 144–147.

Hasenclever, Andreas, Peter Mayer, and Volker Rittberger (1997). *Theories of International Regimes*. Cambridge, UK: Cambridge University Press.

Haynes, Jeffrey (1997). *Democracy and Civil Society in the Third World: Politics and New Political Movements*. Cambridge, UK: Polity.

Hellmann, Gunther (2003a). "Are Dialogue and Synthesis Possible in International Relations? Editor's Note," *International Studies Review* 5 (1): 123.

Hellmann, Gunther (2003b). "In Conclusion: Dialogue and Synthesis in Individual Scholarship and Collective Inquiry," *International Studies Review* 5 (1): 147–150.

Hiley, David, James Bonham, and Richard Shusterman, eds. (1991). *The Interpretive Turn: Philosophy, Science, Culture*. Ithaca, NY: Cornell University Press.

Hoffmann, Matthew (2005). *Ozone Depletion and Climate Change: Constructing a Global Response*. Albany: State University of New York Press.

Hookway, Christopher, and Philip Pettit, eds. (1978). *Action and Interpretation: Studies in the Philosophy of the Social Sciences*. Cambridge, UK: Cambridge University Press.

Hooper, Charlotte (2001). *Manly States: Masculinities, International Relations, and Gender Politics*. New York: Columbia University Press.

Hopf, Ted (1998). "The Promise of Constructivism in International Relations Theory," *International Security* 23 (1): 171–200.

Hopf, Ted (2002). *Social Construction of International Politics: Identities and Foreign Policies, Moscow, 1955 and 1999*. Ithaca, NY: Cornell University Press.

Howell, Martha and Walter Prevenier (2001). *From Reliable Sources: An Introduction to Historical Methods*. Ithaca, NY: Cornell University Press.

Ishay, Micheline (1995). *Internationalism and Its Betrayal*. Minneapolis: University of Minnesota Press.

Jackson, Robert H. (1990). *Quasi-States: Sovereignty, International Relations, and the Third World*. Cambridge, UK: Cambridge University Press.

Jepperson, Ronald L., Alexander Wendt, and Peter J. Katzenstein (1996). "Norms, Identity, and Culture in National Security," in *The Culture of National Security: Norms and Identity in World Politics*, ed Peter J. Katzenstein. New York: Columbia University Press.

Johnston, Hank (2002). "Verification and Proof in Frame and Discourse Analysis," in *Methods of Social Movement Research*, ed. Bert Klandermans and Suzanne Staggenborg. Minneapolis: University of Minnesota Press.

Kaldor, Mary (2003). *Global Civil Society: An Answer to War.* New York: Oxford University Press.

Katzenstein, Peter J., ed. (1996). *The Culture of National Security: Norms and Identity in World Politics.* New York: Columbia University Press.

Katzenstein, Peter J., Robert O. Keohane, and Stephen D. Krasner (1998). "*International Organization* and the Study of World Politics," *International Organization* 52 (4): 645–685.

Keane, John (1998). *Civil Society: Old Images, New Visions.* Stanford, CA: Stanford University Press.

Keck, Margaret E. and Kathryn Sikkink (1998). *Activists beyond Borders: Advocacy Networks in International Politics.* Ithaca, NY: Cornell University Press.

Kinsella, Helen (2005). "Securing the Civilian: Sex and Gender in the Laws of War," in *Power in Global Governance*, ed. Michael Barnett and Raymond Duvall. New York: Cambridge University Press.

Klotz, Audie (1995). *Norms in International Relations: The Struggle against Apartheid.* Ithaca, NY: Cornell University Press.

Klotz, Audie (2001). "Can We Speak a Common Constructivist Language?" in *Constructing International Relations: The Next Generation*, ed. Karin M. Fierke and Knud Erik Jørgensen. Armonk, NY: M.E. Sharpe.

Klotz, Audie (2006). "State Identity in South African Foreign Policy," in *In Full Flight: South African Foreign Policy After Apartheid*, ed. Walter Carlsnaes and Philip Nel. Midrand, South Africa: Institute for Global Dialogue.

Knopf, Jeffrey (1998). *Domestic Society and International Cooperation: The Impact of Protest on US Arms Control Policy.* New York: Cambridge University Press.

Koslowski, Rey (2000). *Migrants and Citizens: Demographic Change in the European State System.* Ithaca, NY: Cornell University Press.

Kratochwil, Friedrich (1989). *Rules, Norms, and Decisions: On the Conditions of Practical and Legal Reasoning in International Relations and Domestic Affairs.* Cambridge, UK: Cambridge University Press.

Kratochwil, Friedrich (2003). "The Monologue of 'Science'," *International Studies Review* 5 (1): 124–128.

Kratochwil, Friedrich V. and John Gerard Ruggie (1986). "International Organization: A State of the Art on an Art of the State," *International Organization* 40 (4): 753–775.

LaCocque, André and David Pellaur (1998). *Thinking Biblically: Exegetical and Hermeneutical Studies.* Chicago: University of Chicago Press.

Laffey, Mark and Jutta Weldes (2005). "Policing and Global Governance,"in *Power in Global Governance*, ed. Michael Barnett and Raymond Duvall. New York: Cambridge University Press.

Larson, Deborah Welch and Alexei Shevchenko (2003). "Shortcut to Greatness: The New Thinking and the Revolution in Soviet Foreign Policy," International Organization 57 (1): 77–109.

Latham, Robert (1997). *The Liberal Moment: Modernity, Security, and the Making of Postwar International Order.* New York: Columbia University Press.

Latour, Bruno (1993). *We Have Never Been Modern.* Cambridge, MA: Harvard University Press.

Lebow, Richard Ned (2003). *The Tragic Vision of Politics: Ethics, Interests, and Orders.* Cambridge and New York: Cambridge University Press.

Lichterman, Paul (2002). "Seeing Structure Happen: Theory-Driven Participant Observation," in *Methods of Social Movement Research*, ed. Bert Klandermans and Suzanne Staggenborg. Minneapolis: University of Minnesota.

Ling, L. H. M. (2002). *Postcolonial International Relations: Conquest and Desire between Asia and the West.* New York: Palgrave.

Little, Daniel (1991). *Varieties of Social Explanation: An Introduction to the Philosophy of Social Science.* Boulder, CO: Westview.

Locher, Birgit and Elizabeth Prügl (2001). "Feminism: Constructivism's Other Pedigree," in *Constructing International Relations: The Next Generation*, ed. Karin M. Fierke and Knud Erik Jørgensen. Armonk, NY: M. E. Sharpe.

Lose, Lars (2001). "Communicative Action and the World of Diplomacy," in *Constructing International Relations: The Next Generation*, ed. Karin M. Fierke and Knud Erik Jørgensen. Armonk, NY: M. E. Sharpe.

Lustick, Ian (1996). "History, Historiography, and Political Science: Multiple Historical Records and the Problem of Selection Bias," *American Political Science Review* 90 (3): 605–618.

Lynch, Cecelia (1999a). *Beyond Appeasement: Interpreting Interwar Peace Movements in World Politics.* Ithaca, NY: Cornell University Press.

Lynch, Cecelia (1999b). "The Promis and Problems of Internationalism," *Global Governance* 5: 83–101.

Lynch, Cecelia (2006). "Critical Interpretation and Interwar Peace Movements: Challenging Dominant Narratives," in *Interpretation and Method: Empirical Research Methods and the Interpretive Turn*, ed. Dvora Yanow and Peregrine Schwartz-Shea. Armonk, NY: M. E. Sharpe.

Mahoney, James and Dietrich Rueschemeyer, eds. (2003). *Comparative Historical Analysis in the Social Sciences.* New York: Cambridge University Press.

Meyer, David S. (1990). *A Winter of Discontent: The Nuclear Freeze and American Politics.* New York: Praeger.

Meyer, John (1979). *National Development and the World System: Educational, Economic, and Political Change 1950-1970.* Chicago: University of Chicago Press.

Milliken, Jennifer (1999). "The Study of Discourse in International Relations: A Critique of Research and Methods," *European Journal of International Relations* 5 (2): 225–254.

Milliken, Jennifer (2001). "Discourse Study: Bringing Rigor to Critical Theory," Karin M. Fierke and Knud Erik Jørgensen, eds, in *Constructing International Relations: The Next Generation,* Armonk and London: M. E. Sharpe.

Monroe, Kristen, ed. (2005). *Perestroika! The Raucous Rebellion in Political Science.* New Haven, CT: Yale University Press.

Monroe, Kristen Renwick, James Hankin, and Renée Bukovchik Van Vechten (2000). "The Psychological Foundations of Identity Politics," *Annual Review of Political Science,* 3: 419–447.

Müller, Harald (2001)."International Relations as Communicative Action," in *Constructing International Relations: The Next Generation,* ed. Karin M. Fierke and Knud Erik Jørgensen. Armonk, NY: M. E. Sharpe.

Müller, Harald (2004). "Arguing, Bargaining, and All That: Communicative Action, Rationalist Theory, and the Logic of Appropriateness," *European Journal of International Relations* 10 (3): 395–435.

Muppidi, Himadeep (2005). "Colonial and Postcolonial Global Governance," in *Power in Global Governance,* ed. Michael Barnett and Raymond Duvall. New York: Cambridge University Press.

Neumann, Iver B. (1996). *Russia and the Idea of Europe: A Study in Identity and International Relations.* London: Routledge.

Neumann, Iver B. (2003). "International Relations as Emergent Bakhtinian Dialogue," *International Studies Review* 5 (1): 137–140.

Neumann, Iver B. (2004). "Deep Structure, Free-Floating Signifier, or Something in Between? Europe's Alterity in Putin's Russia," in *Identity and Global Politics: Empirical and Theoretical Elaborations,* ed. Patricia Goff and Kevin Dunn. New York: Palgrave Macmillan.

Nietzsche, Friedrich (1994). *On the Genealogy of Morality.* Cambridge, UK: Cambridge University Press.

Odell, John (2001). "Case Study Methods in International Political Economy," *International Studies Perspectives* 2 (2): 161–176.

O'Neill, Barry (1999). *Honor, Symbols, and War.* Ann Arbor: University of Michigan Press.

Onuf, Nicholas (1989). *World of Our Making: Rules and Rule in Social Theory and International Relations.* Columbia: University of South Carolina Press.

Onuf, Nicholas (1998). "Constructivism: A User's Manual," in *International Relations in a Constructed World*, ed. Vendulka Kubálková, Nicholas Onuf, and Paul Kowert. Armonk, NY: M. E. Sharpe.

Patterson, Molly and Kristen Renwick Monroe (1998). "Narrative in Political Science," *Annual Review of Political Science*, 1: 315–331.

Peterson, V. Spike (2003). *A Critical Rewriting of Global Political Economy: Integrating Reproductive, Productive, and Virtual Economies*. New York: Routledge.

Peterson, V. Spike and Anne Sisson Runyan (1999). *Global Gender Issues*, 2nd ed. Boulder, CO: Westview.

Philpott, Daniel (2001). *Revolutions in Sovereignty: How Ideas Shaped Modern International Relations*. Princeton, NJ: Princeton University Press.

Pierson, Paul (2004). *Politics in Time: History, Institutions, and Social Analysis*. Princeton, NJ: Princeton University Press.

Polanyi, Karl (1944). *The Great Transformation*. New York: Farrar and Rinehart.

Polkinghorne, Donald (1988). *Narrative Knowing and the Human Sciences*. Albany: State University of New York Press.

Price, Richard (1995). "A Genealogy of the Chemical Weapons Taboo," *International Organization* 49 (1): 73–103.

Price, Richard and Christian Reus-Smit (1998). "Dangerous Liaisons? Critical International Theory and Constructivism," *European Journal of International Relations* 4 (3): 259–294.

Prügl, Elisabeth (1999). *The Global Construction of Gender: Home-Based Work in the Political Economy of the 20th Century*. New York: Columbia University Press.

Rabinow, Paul and William Sullivan, eds. (1979). *Interpretive Social Sciences: A Reader*. Berkeley: University of California Press.

Rae, Heather (2002). *State Identities and the Homogenization of Peoples*. New York: Cambridge University Press.

Ragin, Charles (1994). *Constructing Social Research: The Unity and Diversity of Method*. Thousand Oaks, CA: Pine Forge Press.

Reinharz, Shulamit (1992). *Feminist Methods in Social Research*. New York: Oxford University Press.

Reus-Smit, Christian (1999). *The Moral Purpose of the State: Culture, Social Identity, and Institutional Rationality in International Relations*. Princeton, NJ: Princeton University Press.

Ricoeur, Paul (1981). *Hermeneutics and the Human Sciences: Essays on Language, Action, and Interpretation*. New York: Cambridge University Press.

Ricoeur, Paul (1984). *Time and Narrative, Vol. 1*. Chicago: University of Chicago Press.

Risse, Thomas (2000). "'Let's Argue!': Communicative Action in World Politics," *International Organization* 54 (1): 1–39.

Risse, Thomas (2002). "Constructivism and International Institutions: Toward Conversations Across Paradigms," in *Political Science: The State of the Discipline*, ed. Ira Katznelson and Helen Milner. New York: Norton.

Risse, Thomas and Kathryn Sikkink (1999). "The Socialization of Human Rights Norms into Domestic Practices: Introduction," in *The Power of Human Rights: International Norms and Domestic Change*, ed. Thomas Risse, Stephen C. Ropp, and Kathryn Sikkink. Cambridge, UK: Cambridge University Press.

Robinson, Fiona (1999). *Globalizing Care: Ethics, Feminist Theory, and International Relations*. Boulder, CO: Westview.

Rochon, Thomas R. (1998). *Culture Moves: Ideas, Activism and Changing Values*. Princeton, NJ: Princeton University Press.

Rosenau, Pauline Marie (1992). *Post-Modernism and the Social Sciences: Insights, Inroads, and Intrusions*. Princeton: Princeton University Press.

Rudolph, Susanne Hoeber (2005). "The Imperialism of Categories: Situating Knowledge in a Globalizing World," *Perspectives on Politics* 3 (1 March): 5–14.

Ruggie, John Gerard (1982). "International Regimes, Transactions, and Change: Embedded Liberalism in the Postwar Economic Order," *International Organization* 36 (2): 379–415.

Ruggie, John Gerard (1983). "Continuity and Transformation in the World Polity: Towards a Neorealist Synthesis," *World Politics* 35 (2): 261–285.

Ruggie, John Gerard (1993). "Territoriality and Beyond: Problematizing Modernity in International Relations," *International Organization* 47 (1): 139–174.

Ruggie, John Gerard (1998). *Constructing the World Polity*. New York: Routledge.

Rupert, Mark (1995). *Producing Hegemony: The Politics of Mass Production and American Global Power*. New York: Cambridge University Press.

Rupert, Mark (2000). *Ideologies of Globalization: Contending Visions of a New World Order*. New York: Routledge.

Rupert, Mark (2005). "Class Powers and the Politics of Global Governance," in *Power in Global Governance*, ed. Michael Barnett and Raymond Duvall. New York: Cambridge University Press.

Said, Edward (1978). Orientalism. New York: Vintage.

Salvatore, Armando and Mark LeVine, eds. (2005). *Religion, Social Practice, and Contested Hegemonies: Reconstructing the Public Sphere in Muslim Majority Societies*. New York: Palgrave Macmillan.

Sandoval, Chela (2000). *Methodology of the Oppressed*. Minneapolis: University of Minnesota Press.

Schimmelfennig, Frank (2003). *The EU, NATO and the Integration of Europe.* New York: Cambridge University Press.

Schmitz, Hans Peter (2006). *Transnational Mobilization and Domestic Regime Change: Africa in Comparative Perspective.* New York: Palgrave Macmillan.

Schön, Donald and Martin Rein (1994). *Frame Reflection: Toward the Resolution of Intractable Policy Controversies.* New York: Basic Books.

Scott, James (1990). *Domination and the Arts of Resistance: Hidden Transcripts.* New Haven, CT: Yale University Press.

Searle, John (1969). *Speech Acts: An Essay in the Philosophy of Language.* Cambridge, UK: Cambridge University Press.

Sewell, William H., Jr. (2001). "Whatever Happened to the 'Social' in Social History?" in *Schools of Thought: Twenty-five Years of Interpretive Social Science,* ed. Joan W. Scott and Debra Keates. Princeton, NJ: Princeton University Press.

Skinner, Quentin, ed. (1985). *The Return of Grand Theory in the Human Sciences.* New York: Cambridge University Press.

Snow, David A. and Robert D. Benford (1988). "Ideology, Frame Resonance, and Participant Mobilization," in *International Social Movement Research, vol. 1, From Structure to Action: Comparing Social Movement Research Across Cultures,* ed. Bert Klandermans, Hanspeter Kriesi, and Sidney Tarrow. Greenwich, CT: JAI Press.

Spivak, Gayatri (1987). *In Other Worlds: Essays in Cultural Politics.* New York: Methuen.

Struett, Michael (2005). "The Politics of Constructing the International Criminal Court." Unpublished Ph.D. dissertation, University of California, Irvine.

Suganami, Hidemi (1999). "Agents, Structures, Narratives," *European Journal of International Relations* 5 (3): 365–386.

Sylvester, Christine (1994). *Feminist Theory and International Relations in a Postmodern Era.* Cambridge, UK: Cambridge University Press.

Taylor, Charles (2001). "Modernity and Identity," in *Schools of Thought: Twenty-Five Years of Interpretive Social Science,* ed. Joan W. Scott and Debra Keats. Princeton, NJ: Princeton University Press.

Tetlock, Philip and Aaron Belkin (1996). *Counterfactual Thought Experiments in World Politics: Logical, Methodological, and Psychological Perspectives.* Princeton, NJ: Princeton University Press.

Thomas, Daniel C. (2001). *The Helsinki Effect: International Norms, Human Rights, and the Demise of Communism.* Princeton, NJ: Princeton University Press.

Tickner, J. Ann (1992). *Gender in International Relations: Feminist Perspectives on Achieving Global Security.* New York: Columbia University Press.

Tickner, J. Ann (2001). *Gendering World Politics: Issues and Approaches in the Post-Cold War Era.* New York: Columbia University Press.

Tilly, Charles (1984). *Big Structures, Large Processes, Huge Comparisons.* New York: Russell Sage Foundation.

Todorov, Tzvetan (1984). *The Conquest of America: The Question of the Other.* New York: Harper and Row.

True, Jacqui (2001). *Gender, Globalization, and Postsocialism: The Czech Republic after Communism.* New York: Columbia University Press.

Waever, Ole (1998). "The Sociology of a Not So International Discipline: American and European Developments in International Relations," *International Organization* 52 (4): 687–727.

Walker, R. B. J. (1993). *Inside/Outside: International Relations as Political Theory.* Cambridge, UK: Cambridge University Press.

Wapner, Paul (1996). *Environmental Activism and World Civic Politics.* Albany: State University of New York Press.

Weber, Cynthia (1995). *Simulating Sovereignty: Intervention, the State and Symbolic Exchange.* Cambridge: Cambridge University Press.

Weber, Max (1949). *Methodology of the Social Sciences,* trans. and ed. Edward A. Shils and Henry A. Finch. Glencoe, IL: Free Press.

Weber, Max (1963). *The Sociology of Religion.* Boston: Beacon Press.

Weldes, Jutta (1999). *Constructing National Interests: The United States and the Cuban Missile Crisis.* Minneapolis: University of Minnesota Press.

Weldes, Jutta, Mark Laffey, Hugh Gusterson, and Raymond Duvall, eds. (1999). *Cultures of Insecurity: States, Communities, and the Production of Danger.* Minneapolis: University of Minnesota Press.

Wendt, Alexander (1987). "The Agent-Structure Problem in International Relations Theory," *International Organization* 41 (3): 335–370.

Wendt, Alexander (1999). *Social Theory of International Relations.* Cambridge, UK: Cambridge University Press.

Wendt, Alexander and Raymond Duvall (1989). "Institutions and International Order," in Global Changes and Theoretical Challenges, ed. Ernst-Otto Czempiel and James N. Rosenau. New York: Macmillan.

White, Hayden (1987). *The Content of the Form: Narrative Discourse and Historical Representation.* Baltimore, MD: Johns Hopkins University Press.

Wiarda, Howard J. (2003). *Civil Society: The American Model and Third World Development.* Boulder, CO: Westview.

Wiener, Antje (1998). *"European" Citizenship Practice: Building Institutions of a Non-State.* Boulder, CO: Westview.

Wilmer, Franke (2002). *The Social Construction of Man, the State, and War: Identity, Conflict, and Violence in the Former Yugoslavia.* New York: Routledge.

Winch, Peter (1958). *The Idea of a Social Science and Its Relation to Philosophy*. London: Routledge and Paul.

Wittgenstein, Ludwig (1958). *Philosophical Investigations*. Oxford: Blackwell.

Wolfers, Arnold (1962). *Discord and Collaboration: Essays on International Politics*. Baltimore, MD: Johns Hopkins University Press.

Yanow, Dvora, and Peregrine Schwartz-Shea, eds. (2006). *Interpretation and Method: Empirical Research Methods and the Interpretive Turn*. Armonk, NY: M. E. Sharpe.

# Index

# About the Authors

**Audie Klotz** is Associate Professor of Political Science at the Maxwell School of Syracuse University, where she teaches international relations theory and qualitative methods, among other courses. She is the author of *Norms in International Relations: The Struggle against Apartheid* (Cornell 1995), which won the Furniss Prize in international security studies. Her work has also appeared in *International Organization, Review of International Studies, Third World Quarterly*, and *European Journal of International Relations*, among other journals and edited collections, and she is currently working on comparative responses to global migration.

**Cecelia Lynch** is Associate Professor of Political Science at the University of California, Irvine. Her books include *Beyond Appeasement: Interpreting Interwar Peace Movements in World Politics* (Cornell 1999), which won the Furniss Prize in international security studies and the Myrna Bernath Prize of the Society of Historians of American Foreign Relations. Her work on peace movements, religion, interpretive methods, and IR theory has appeared in *Ethics & International Affairs, Millenium, Global Governance,* and *Alternatives*, as well as other journals and books. She is currently funded by an Andrew Mellon Foundation fellowship to work on inter-faith religious ethics in world politics.

# STRATEGIES FOR RESEARCH
## in Constructivist International Relations

# International Relations in a Constructed World

**Commonsense Constructivism, or
The Making of World Affairs**
*Ralph Pettman*

**Constructing International Relations:
The Next Generation**
*Karin M. Fierke and Knud Erik Jørgensen, editors*

**Constructing Human Rights in the Age of Globalization**
*Mahmood Monshipouri, Neil Englehart, Andrew J. Nathan,
and Kavita Philip, editors*

**Constructivism and Comparative Politics**
*Daniel M. Green, editor*

**Foreign Policy in a Constructed World**
*Vendulka Kubálková, editor*

**International Relations in a Constructed World**
*Vendulka Kubálková, Nicholas Onuf, and Paul Kowert, editors*

**Language, Agency, and Politics in a Constructed World**
*François Debrix, editor*

**Strategies for Research in Constructivist International Relations**
*Audie Koltz and Cecelia Lynch*

---

### Series Editors

Vendulka Kubálková, *University of Miami*
Nicholas Onuf, *Florida International University*
Ralph Pettman, *Victoria University of Wellington*

---

### Editorial Advisory Board